COMMUNITY BASED INSTRUCTION
Special Education Workbook

Restaurant Skill: Enter Respectfully

Thomas is going to Burger Village with his class today. His goal is to practice entering the restaurant respectfully. Last time he went on a community outing, Thomas was so excited that he ran up to the door. He made the mistake of pushing it open quickly and bumped into an older lady who was carrying her tray. She spilled her food and Thomas felt awful. This time, Thomas will be sure to walk calmly up to the door and look around before he opens it. Thomas wants to make sure he enters the restaurant as respectfully as possible.

Part A: Check Each Box as you Complete the Task

☐ Read the Story
☐ Circle the word   respectfully
☐ Trace & Write the word below

respectfully

Part B: Fill in the Blank

1. Who is this story about?

2. What is Thomas' goal for his outing?

3. Where is Thomas going with his class?

©Check in with Mrs G LLC 2021-present

Restaurant Skill: Enter Respectfully

Part C: Write the Main Idea of the Story

Part D: Write One Supporting Detail from the Story

Restaurant Self Assessment

Think about your outing to the restaurant. How did you do?

Date:

Restaurant Name:

Rate yourself on each skill you practiced while you were there.

SKILL	5 Points	3 Points	1 Point
Entered the Restaurant Respectfully	○ Walked calmly ○ Used eye contact ○ Inside voice volume ○ Waited patiently ○ Friendly	○ Walked quickly ○ Some eye contact ○ Talked loudly ○ Waited ○ Somewhat friendly	○ Ran ○ No eye contact ○ Yelled or was disruptive ○ Impatient ○ Unfriendly
Read the Menu	○ Opened the menu ○ Read the list of items ○ Chose an item independently ○ Evaluated cost & stayed within budget	○ Opened the menu with reminders ○ Asked for an item without checking the menu ○ Chose an item with support ○ Chose something I could not afford	○ Did not look at the menu ○ Asked an adult to choose food ○ Did not consider the cost
Ordered my Food	○ Made eye contact ○ Spoke clearly ○ Appropriate volume ○ Extremely polite (said Please/ Thank You)	○ Some eye contact ○ Order was unclear ○ Spoke too quietly or too loudly ○ Somewhat polite	○ No eye contact ○ Did not order on my own ○ Impolite or demanding
Paid for my Food	○ Had my money organized & ready ○ Gave an appropriate amount ○ Counted my change ○ Kept my receipt in a safe place	○ Had my money ○ Gave an amount larger than what was owed ○ Took my change ○ Took my receipt	○ Forgot my money ○ Gave less than what was owed ○ Did not take my change ○ Did not take my receipt
Left Politely	○ Walked calmly ○ Used eye contact ○ Inside voice volume ○ Said thank you ○ Friendly ○ Held the door open for someone	○ Walked quickly ○ Some eye contact ○ Talked loudly ○ Said thank you ○ Somewhat friendly	○ Ran ○ No eye contact ○ Yelled or was disruptive ○ Unfriendly

Student Name:

Today, I feel I earned Total Points: ___/25

©KrystalGriffith2018-present Check in with Mrs G

Instructions for Use

Every student is unique in their needs and ability level. Therefore, this content is designed to be easily broken into digestible parts. Here is a suggested session outline for using this community based instruction workbook for students in special education. From one teacher to another, thank you for doing the most important job on the planet.
Happy teaching!

Complete the following sessions for each of the five skills within a designated topic. The topics included in this workbook are:

Restaurant Skills
Community Center Skills
Public Transportation Skills
Library Skills
Shopping Skills
Community Social Skills

Warm Up for each Topic:
Warm up by introducing the topic and associated vocabulary using the skill list & student warm up page

Skill Session I:
Develop reading fluency by having student read the example passage aloud, increase comprehension by having student work through the corresponding questions *Note, this often takes two days in my classroom

Skill Session 2:
Repeat instructions from session one for the second example passage and corresponding set of comprehension questions

Skill Session 3:
Have student demonstrate knowledge by responding to journal prompts in written and picture format

Topic Conclusion:
Facilitate a meaning making conversation where students will connect learning to their own lives using the Make a Connection Page

Extended Learning:
Review the included rubric for each topic and use it to set personal goals for community based outings with each student. Upon completion of the outing, students should use the rubric to monitor their own progress toward a community based goal. This can be a great tool to use to track social and emotional data to include on an IEP.

*Blackline masters of the self-reflection rubrics for each topic have been included in the back of this book.

Community Based Instruction

Restaurant Skills

Enter Respectfully

Read the Menu

Order your Food

Pay

Leave Politely

Community Based Instruction

Warm Up: Restaurant

What is a restaurant?

➡️

Something I enjoy about going to restaurants...

➡️

One restaurant I have been to...

One thing I do not enjoy about going to restaurants is...

➡️

⬇️

Here are a few skills I think people need to have to eat at a restaurant:

Restaurant Skill: Enter Respectfully

Thomas is going to Burger Village with his class today. His goal is to practice entering the restaurant respectfully. Last time he went on a community outing, Thomas was so excited he ran up to the door.

Then he made the mistake of pushing it open too quickly and bumped into an older woman who was carrying her tray. She spilled her food and Thomas felt awful.

This time, Thomas will be sure to walk calmly up to the door and look around before he opens it. Thomas wants to make sure he enters the restaurant as respectfully as possible.

Part A: Check Each Box as you Complete the Task

❑ **Read the Story**
❑ **Circle the word** respectfully **in the story**
❑ **Trace & Write the word below:**

respectfully _____

Part B: Fill in the Blank

1. **Who is this story about?**

_____

2. **What is Thomas' goal for his outing?**

_____

3. **Where is Thomas going with his class today?**

_____

Part C: Write the Main Idea of the Story

_____

_____

_____

_____

_____

Part D: Write One Supporting Detail from the Story

_____

_____

_____

_____

Part E: Do you think entering a restaurant respectfully is an important skill? Why or why not?

_____

_____

_____

_____

_____

_____

_____

_____

_____

_____

Restaurant Skill: Enter Respectfully

Harper is happy to be at Shale Town with her classmates. She's hungry and Shale Town is her favorite restaurant. When the door opens, she sees that there is a long line of people waiting to order.

Harper is so frustrated she wants to yell! Her teacher tells Harper to take a deep breath and says that being impatient is not helpful. Harper looks at the people behind the counter and notices that they are working as hard as they can.

She decides to put on a friendly smile. Harper waits respectfully with her teacher until it is her turn to order.

Part A: Check Each Box as you Complete the Task

❑   **Read the Story**
❑   **Circle the word** (respectfully) **in the story**
❑   **Trace & Write the word below:**

respectfully _____ _____

Part B: Fill in the Blank

1. **Who is this story about?**

   _____

2. **Why does Harper want to yell?**

   _____
   _____
   _____
   _____

Part C: Write the Main Idea of the Story

_____

_____

_____

_____

_____

Part D: Write One Supporting Detail from the Story

_____

_____

_____

_____

_____

Part E: Deepen your Understanding

What is Harper's favorite restaurant?

a. McDandys

b. The Pizza Shack

c. Shakes & Stuff

d. Shale Town

How does Harper calm down?

a. She waits in the car

b. She takes a deep breath

c. She uses a fidget

d. She goes on a run

What does it sound like to walk into a restaurant in a respectful way?

_____

_____

_____

_____

_____

_____

_____

_____

_____

_____

_____

_____

Here is a picture of what it looks like to enter a restaurant in a respectful way:

Restaurant Skill: Read the Menu

Avery is a picky eater. It usually takes her a long time to find something she wants to eat. So, when Avery sits down at the restaurant with her friends, she reads the menu right away.

She wants as much time as possible to make a decision about what she would like to order. When her friends try to talk to her, Avery says politely, "I need a few minutes to read the menu please."

Her friends wait patiently as Avery reads each item on the menu. She decides to order a chicken sandwich with no mayonnaise, then goes back to talking with her friends. When the waiter comes over, Avery is ready to order.

Part A: Check Each Box as you Complete the Task

❑　　　Read the Story
❑　　　Circle the word　(reads)　in the story
❑　　　Trace & Write the word below:

_____ reads _____　　_____

Part B: Fill in the Blank

1. Who is this story about?

_____

2. What is a "picky eater"?

_____

3. What did Avery decide to order?

_____

Part C: Write the Main Idea of the Story

_____

_____

_____

_____

_____

Part D: Write One Supporting Detail from the Story

_____

_____

_____

_____

_____

Part E: Why did Avery think it was important to read her menu right away?

_____

_____

_____

_____

_____

_____

_____

_____

_____

Restaurant Skill: Read the Menu

Luke was at Foodie Express with his friends. He was starving! Everything on the menu looked delicious. Luke wanted to order a salad, burger, fries, broccoli, and a chocolate milkshake with whip cream. But he knew he only had $10.00 in his wallet and he wanted to make sure her could afford it.

Luke added up each item and discovered it would cost $13.00. He realized he did not have enough to buy everything. So, Luke decided not to order fries or a milkshake. He added up the cost again and was so happy when he found that his new total would be $8.00. Luke had enough money! Luke used the prices on the menu to determine what he could afford to order.

Part A: Check Each Box as you Complete the Task

☐ **Read the Story**
☐ **Circle the word** (menu) **in the story**
☐ **Trace & Write the word below:**

menu

------------------------------   ------------------------------

Part B: Fill in the Blank

1. **Who is this story about?**

_____

2. **Why didn't Luke order fries or a milkshake?**

_____

_____

_____

_____

Part C: Write the Main Idea of the Story

_____

_____

_____

_____

_____

Part D: Write One Supporting Detail from the Story

_____

_____

_____

_____

_____

Part E: Deepen your Understanding

Luke had $10.00 in his wallet. How much more money did he need to buy all of the items he wanted?

a. $13.00

b. $1.00

c. $3.00

d. $20.00

How did Luke know he did not have enough money to buy all of the items he wanted?

a. He added up the cost of items

b. He guessed

c. He asked his teacher

d. He waited until the bill came

How can reading the menu right away help you decide
what you want to eat?

_____

_____

_____

_____

_____

_____

_____

_____

_____

_____

_____

_____

My sketch of a restaurant:

Restaurant Skill: Order Food

Mila went on an outing with her class. For Mila, the hardest part about outings is having to talk to people. Today, she had a goal of ordering her food independently.

When the waiter came to her table, Mila took a deep breath and looked right at the waiter. She smiled politely and said, "I would like to order the soup please." She used a voice that was loud enough for him to hear but not so loud it hurt his ears. The waiter asked Mila whether or not she wanted bread. Mila got a little nervous because she was not prepared to answer any questions, but she nodded her head in a friendly way. Mila was proud of herself for ordering! Next time, Mila has a goal of answering questions in a confident way.

Part A: Check Each Box as you Complete the Task

❑   **Read the Story**
❑   **Circle the word   order   in the story**
❑   **Trace & Write the word below:**

order
-------------------------   -------------------------

Part B: Fill in the Blank

1. **Who is this story about?**

_____

2. **What is Mila's goal today?**

_____

3. **What is Mila's goal for next time?**

_____

Part C: Write the Main Idea of the Story

_____

_____

_____

_____

_____

Part D: Write One Supporting Detail from the Story

_____

_____

_____

_____

_____

Part E: Why do you think Mila took a deep breath before she ordered her food?

_____

_____

_____

_____

_____

_____

_____

_____

_____

_____

Restaurant Skill: Order Food

Mathew knows that being polite is important when in the community. Today, Matthew is at Coffee Land and is ordering a white mocha. One of the things he likes best about this coffee shop is that the baristas are always so friendly.

Matthew is friendly too, even when there is a long line. When they ask his name to write it on the cup, Matthew tells them and even helps them spell it. He is sure to say please when ordering his white mocha and thank you when he picks it up. Matthew knows that it makes everyone's day better when he has a polite and positive attitude when ordering his coffee.

Part A: Check Each Box as you Complete the Task

- ☐ **Read the Story**
- ☐ **Circle the word** (order) **in the story**
- ☐ **Trace & Write the word below:**

order _____ _____

Part B: Fill in the Blank

1. Who is this story about?

   _____

2. What is Matthew ordering?

   _____

3. Why does Matthew spell his name for the baristas?

   _____

Part C: Write the Main Idea of the Story

_____

_____

_____

_____

_____

Part D: Write One Supporting Detail from the Story

_____

_____

_____

_____

_____

Part E: Why do you think Matthew is polite even when there is a long line?

_____

_____

_____

_____

_____

_____

_____

_____

_____

23

Why is it important to find out how much each item on the menu costs before you choose what you will order?

_____

_____

_____

_____

_____

_____

_____

_____

_____

_____

_____

_____

_____

_____

_____

My sketch of a menu of my favorite things to eat:

Menu

Restaurant Skill: Pay the Bill

Aria was getting ready for an outing to Souptacular. Aria knew that she would need to pay for her own lunch. She checked her wallet because she wanted to find out how much money she had to spend.

Aria's money was crumpled and thrown into her backpack. She shook her bag and heard change jingling. Aria had money mixed with receipts, garbage, and even homework. That made it hard to count!

So, Aria took everything out of her backpack, organized her money and then counted it. She put her money neatly into her wallet. At Souptacular she knew where her money was and how much she had to spend.

Part A: Check Each Box as you Complete the Task

❑ Read the Story
❑ Circle the word ⬭pay⬭ in the story
❑ Trace & Write the word below:

-------------- pay -------------- --------------------------

Part B: Fill in the Blank

1. Who is this story about?

_____

2. What made it difficult for Aria to count her money?

_____

3. Why did Aria need to know how much money she had?

_____

Part C: Write the Main Idea of the Story

_____

_____

_____

_____

_____

Part D: Write One Supporting Detail from the Story

_____

_____

_____

_____

_____

Part E: Deepen your Understanding

What was Aria buying?

a. Movies

b. Popcorn

c. Books

d. Lunch

Where did Aria decide to keep her money after she organized it?

a. In her backpack

b. With her teacher

c. In her wallet

d. In her desk

Restaurant Skill: Pay the Bill

Adam was at the mall. He waited in line at the food court with his tray of pizza and chips. He knew he needed to pay before he found a table and ate.

When he got up to the cashier, Adam took out his wallet. His total was $6.75. He handed a ten dollar bill to the cashier. The cashier took it and made change for Adam. Adam counted the change to make sure it was the correct amount.

Adam knew that cashiers sometimes make mistakes too so, he always double checked. Adam's change was $3.25, the correct amount! Adam smiled, thanked the cashier, and tucked his change into his wallet.

Part A: Check Each Box as you Complete the Task

☐   **Read the Story**
☐   **Circle the word   pay   in the story**
☐   **Trace & Write the word below:**

---------- pay ----------   -------------------------

Part B: Fill in the Blank

1. **Who is this story about?**

   _____

2. **Where is Adam?**

   _____

3. **How much change did Adam receive?**

   _____

Part C: Write the Main Idea of the Story

_____

_____

_____

_____

_____

Part D: Write One Supporting Detail from the Story

_____

_____

_____

_____

_____

Part E: Why do you think Adam counted the change he was handed by the cashier?

_____

_____

_____

_____

_____

_____

_____

_____

_____

Why is it important to keep your money organized in your wallet?

_____

_____

_____

_____

_____

_____

_____

_____

_____

_____

_____

_____

My sketch of an unorganized wallet:

My sketch of an organized wallet:

Restaurant Skill: Leave Politely

When Nora and Carter finished their lunch at Taco Table, they paid their bill and got up calmly. The two friends walked toward the exit. The restaurant hostess noticed them heading for the door and walked quickly to open it for them.

On the way out, the hostess asked cheerfully, "How was everything?"

Nora responded with a smile, "it was great, thanks!"

Carter looked directly out of the window at the parking lot and did not acknowledge the hostess' question. Nora and Carter walked happily out through the door talking quietly with one another.

Part A: Check Each Box as you Complete the Task

❑   **Read the Story**
❑   **Circle the word** (politely) **in the story**
❑   **Trace & Write the word below:**

_____politely_____   _____

Part B: Fill in the Blank

1. **Who is this story about?**

   _____

2. **Where did Nora and Carter eat lunch?**

   _____

3. **What is a restaurant hostess?**

   _____

Part C: Write the Main Idea of the Story

_____

_____

_____

_____

_____

Part D: Write One Supporting Detail from the Story

_____

_____

_____

_____

_____

Part E: Deepen your Understanding

Did Nora leave the restaurant politely? Explain	Did Carter leave the restaurant politely? Explain.
_____	_____
_____	_____
_____	_____
_____	_____
_____	_____
_____	_____
_____	_____

Restaurant Skill: Leave Politely

Caroline went to Joaquin's Deli with her class today. Her goal was to practice leaving the restaurant in a polite way. Usually, Caroline got tired after she ate and wanted to leave as soon a possible, even when some of her classmates were not done eating. Caroline does not want to talk to anyone when she is full. But today, she wanted to meet her goal of being polite. Caroline knows that being unfriendly, impatient, and staring at her phone is not polite. Today after she ate, Caroline waited patiently for her classmates. Then she walked to the door with a friendly smile on her face. Caroline saw an older couple walking in and held the door open for them. Caroline met her goal!

<u>Part A:</u> Check Each Box as you Complete the Task

- ❏ **Read the Story**
- ❏ **Circle the word** (leaving) **in the story**
- ❏ **Trace & Write the word below:**

leaving

------------------------   ------------------------

<u>Part B:</u> Fill in the Blank

1. **Who is this story about?**

_____

2. **What does Caroline usually do that is impolite?**

_____

_____

_____

_____

Part C: Write the Main Idea of the Story

_____

_____

_____

_____

_____

Part D: Write One Supporting Detail from the Story

_____

_____

_____

_____

Part E: Deepen your Understanding

When does Caroline not want to talk to anyone?

a. When she is full

b. When she is hungry

c. When she needs to take a nap

d. When she is doing homework

What did Caroline do after she finished her meal?

a. Talk on her phone

b. Leave the restaurant

c. Wait patiently

d. Take a nap on the bus

How do you think other people feel when you leave a restaurant in a polite way?

_____

_____

_____

_____

_____

_____

_____

_____

_____

_____

_____

_____

_____

My sketch what I would order for breakfast at a restaurant:

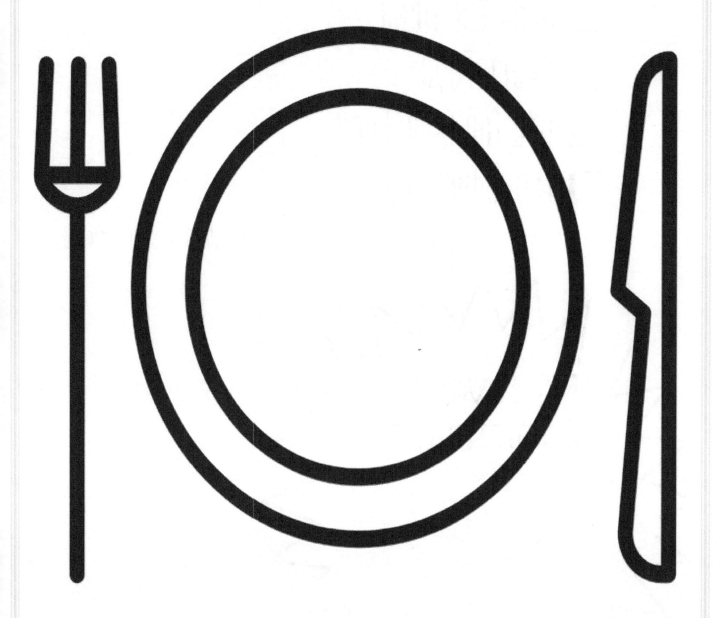

Restaurant Skills

Check point! Review each skill.

- ☐ Enter the Restaurant Respectfully
- ☐ Read the Menu
- ☐ Order Food
- ☐ Pay for your Food
- ☐ Leave Politely

Here is what I know about going to restaurants:

My favorite Restaurant

One restaurant skill I am already good at is...

Restaurant Skills I need to Practice:

○

○

○

○

○

○

○

My favorite kind of food to eat at a restaurant...

A restaurant I hope to go to is...

Think about your outing to the restaurant. How did you do?

Rate yourself on each skill you practiced while you were there.

Date:

Restaurant Name:

SKILL	5 Points	3 Points	1 Point
Entered the Restaurant Respectfully	○ Walked calmly ○ Used eye contact ○ Inside voice volume ○ Waited patiently ○ Friendly	○ Walked quickly ○ Some eye contact ○ Talked loudly ○ Waited ○ Somewhat friendly	○ Ran ○ No eye contact ○ Yelled or was disruptive ○ Impatient ○ Unfriendly
Read the Menu	○ Opened the menu ○ Read the list of items ○ Chose an item independently ○ Evaluated cost & stayed within budget	○ Opened the menu with reminders ○ Asked for an item without checking the menu ○ Chose an item with support ○ Chose something I could not afford	○ Did not look at the menu ○ Asked an adult to choose food ○ Did not consider the cost
Ordered my Food	○ Made eye contact ○ Spoke clearly ○ Appropriate volume ○ Extremely polite (said Please/ Thank You)	○ Some eye contact ○ Order was unclear ○ Spoke too quietly or too loudly ○ Somewhat polite	○ No eye contact ○ Did not order on my own ○ Impolite or demanding
Paid for my Food	○ Had my money organized & ready ○ Gave an appropriate amount ○ Counted my change ○ Kept my receipt in a safe place	○ Had my money ○ Gave an amount larger than what was owed ○ Took my change ○ Took my receipt	○ Forgot my money ○ Gave less than what was owed ○ Did not take my change ○ Did not take my receipt
Left Politely	○ Walked calmly ○ Used eye contact ○ Inside voice volume ○ Said thank you ○ Friendly ○ Held the door open for someone	○ Walked quickly ○ Some eye contact ○ Talked loudly ○ Said thank you ○ Somewhat friendly	○ Ran ○ No eye contact ○ Yelled or was disruptive ○ Unfriendly

Student Name:

Today, I feel I earned

Total Points: ___ /25

Student Rubric Reflection: Restaurant

Looking at my rubric I see...

It is **important** to learn what to do at a **restaurant** because...

I am proud of:

_____

_____

_____

_____

_____

_____

_____

_____

I need to keep working on:

_____

_____

_____

_____

_____

_____

_____

Community Based Instruction

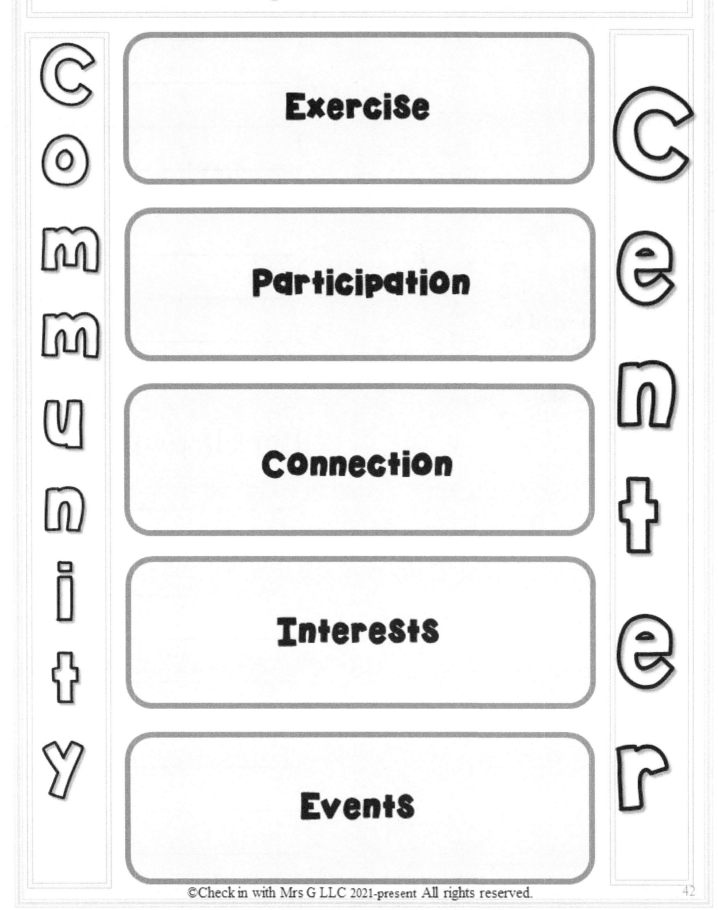

Community

Center

Exercise

Participation

Connection

Interests

Events

Community Based Instruction

Warm Up: Community Center

Have you ever been to a community center?

Here are a few things I already know about community centers...

IS there a community center in your town or city?

Yes **No**

Something that makes me nervous or excited about going to a community center is...

Here is a question I have about community centers:

Community Center: Exercise

Tuesday is Jose's favorite day of the week because on Tuesdays his class goes to the community center. He loves to exercise in the pool when they are there. His teacher always reminds him to bring swimming trunks and a towel from home.

When they arrive at the community center, Jose uses the locker room to change. He puts his clothes into a locker and locks it. Then, he heads to the pool. Jose swims laps and stretches out afterwards. His mind feels clear and his muscles feel strong when he makes the time to exercise.

Part A: Check Each Box as you Complete the Task

❑   Read the Story
❑   Circle the word exercise in the story
❑   Trace & Write the word below:

exercise _____

Part B: Fill in the Blank

1. Who is this story about?

   _____

2. What does Jose like to do at the community center?

   _____

3. What does Jose bring with him to school on Tuesdays?

   _____

Part C: Write the Main Idea of the Story

_____

_____

_____

_____

_____

Part D: Write One Supporting Detail from the Story

_____

_____

_____

_____

_____

Part E: Deepen your Understanding

What day of the week does Jose go to the community center?	How does Jose feel when he is done swimming?
a. Monday	a. Frustrated
b. Tuesday	b. Excited
c. Wednesday	c. Strong
d. Thursday	d. Angry

Community Center: Exercise

The community center by Luna's house has many group exercise classes. She likes to go after work. Normally Luna spends her time on stationary bikes, dancing, or lifting weights. But today, she is going to a boxing class.

Luna will be sure to bring a towel and a water bottle so she can stay hydrated while she works out. Luna loves to challenge herself with new types of exercise. Exercise helps Luna think more clearly and she thinks it is fun. That is why Luna loves the community center. There are so many ways to get a good workout!

Part A: Check Each Box as you Complete the Task

❑ Read the Story
❑ Circle the word (exercise) in the story
❑ Trace & Write the word below:

exercise _____ _____

Part B: Fill in the Blank

1. Who is this story about?

_____

2. What are some types of exercise Luna has tried?

_____

3. When does Luna like to go to the community center?

_____

Part C: Write the Main Idea of the Story

_____

_____

_____

_____

_____

Part D: Write One Supporting Detail from the Story

_____

_____

_____

_____

_____

Part E: Deepen your Understanding

What type of exercise class is Luna going to today?

a. Cycling

b. Dancing

c. Boxing

d. Swimming

What does Luna bring with her to the community center?

a. Books

b. Towel

c. Change of Clothes

d. Homework

Do you think it is important to exercise? Explain how a community center can help you exercise.

_____

_____

_____

_____

_____

_____

_____

_____

_____

_____

_____

_____

My sketch of one way to exercise at a community center:

Community Center: Participation

When Riley goes to the community center, she always makes it her goal to participate. She joins classes, tries new activities and plays group games.

The community center in her town has pool tables. Riley loves to play pool with kids that are around her age. She also likes when the community center has the gym open for basketball.

When the community center is open, Riley spends her free time there making new friends and participating in new activities.

Part A: Check Each Box as you Complete the Task

☐   Read the Story
☐   Circle the word (participate) in the story
☐   Trace & Write the word below:

participate _____   _____

Part B: Fill in the Blank

1. Who is this story about?

   _____

2. What goal does Riley have?

   _____

3. How does Riley participate at the community center?

   _____

Community Center: Participation

Part C: Write the Main Idea of the Story

_____

_____

_____

_____

_____

Part D: Write One Supporting Detail from the Story

_____

_____

_____

_____

_____

Part E: Deepen your Understanding

Which of these activities does Riley's community center not have?	How do you think Riley feels about the community center?
a. Pool Tables	_____
b. Gym	_____
c. Soccer Field	_____
d. Basketball Court	_____

Community Center: Participation

Greyson sees a group of boys making towers out of Legos at his local community center. He wants to join them but he's feeling a little shy. Greyson makes sure his body language is open and that he makes friendly eye contact with everyone.

His positive attitude makes him seem more approachable. Then, Greyson takes a deep breath, walks up to the group and says hello. He asks if he can join them. They say yes! Even though he feels awkward at first, Greyson knows it is worth it. Participating in activities with new friends is Greyson's favorite part of going to the community center.

Part A: Check Each Box as you Complete the Task

☐   **Read the Story**
☐   **Circle the word** (participating) **in the story**
☐   **Trace & Write the word below:**

participating   ----------------------

Part B: Fill in the Blank

1. Who is this story about?

   _____

2. What activity does Greyson want to participate in?

   _____

3. How does Greyson feel about joining the group?

   _____

Part C: Write the Main Idea of the Story

_____

_____

_____

_____

_____

Part D: Write One Supporting Detail from the Story

_____

_____

_____

_____

_____

Part E: Deepen your Understanding

What makes Greyson feel unsure?	Why is body language important when you want to participate in a group?
a. How to approach a group	_____
	_____
	_____
b. How to build a Lego tower	_____
	_____
c. Whether or not he wants to join	_____
	_____
d. Where he left his backpack	_____

Participating in activities or events at a community center can look different for everyone. What are some ways you can participate at the community center in your town?

_____

_____

_____

_____

_____

_____

_____

_____

_____

_____

_____

_____

My sketch of friendly body language:

Community Center: Connection

One of the best things about going to a community center is the opportunity for connection. Ava was unsure of what to do on her class outing to the community center. She spent time reading a list of activities and found a group that worked on learning to code.

Ava loved to learn about robotics and coding! She asked her mom to take her to the class on Thursday night. When she got there, Ava connected with other kids her age who were interested in the same types of technology activities. She even found a partner to help build her next robot!

Part A: Check Each Box as you Complete the Task

❑   Read the Story
❑   Circle the word (connection) in the story
❑   Trace & Write the word below:

connection   _____

Part B: Fill in the Blank

1. Who is this story about?

    _____

2. What are Ava's interests?

    _____

3. Where did she find a partner to help her build a robot?

    _____

Part C: Write the Main Idea of the Story

_____

_____

_____

_____

_____

Part D: Write One Supporting Detail from the Story

_____

_____

_____

_____

_____

Part E: Deepen your Understanding

How did Ava learn about the coding class?

a. She saw it online

b. She read about it at the community center

c. She asked her mom about classes

d. Her teacher told her about it

When is robotics class?

a. During school

b. 10:00am

c. Tuesday nights

d. Thursday nights

Community Center: Connection

When Charles is at the community center, he loves to connect with students his own age who go to public schools. Charles is home schooled by his mom and loves making new friends.

The community center is a great place for him to meet new friends who like reading, football and video games just like he does. Charles tries to go at least three afternoons each week. The connections Charles makes while at the community center often turn into friendships. Charles is thankful that he lives so close he can walk!

Part A: Check Each Box as you Complete the Task

❑   Read the Story
❑   Circle the word ⟨connect⟩ in the story
❑   Trace & Write the word below:

__connect__   _____

Part B: Fill in the Blank

1. Who is this story about?

   _____

2. How does Charles get to the community center?

   _____

3. When does Charles go to the community center?

   _____

Part C: Write the Main Idea of the Story

_____

_____

_____

_____

_____

Part D: Write One Supporting Detail from the Story

_____

_____

_____

_____

_____

Part E: Deepen your Understanding

Which of these is not an interest that Charles has?

a. Football

b. Video Games

c. Soccer

d. Books

What is unique about Charles' school?

_____

_____

_____

_____

_____

_____

_____

_____

_____

_____

How can going to a class that you are interested in at a community center help you connect with new friends?

_____

_____

_____

_____

_____

_____

_____

_____

_____

_____

_____

_____

My sketch of a class I would like to attend:

Community Center: Interests

Camilla knows that no matter what your interests, you will be able to find something you enjoy participating in at the community center. Camilla knows this because last year she did not want to go to the community center on her class outings.

She thought that it would be boring. That was before she started getting involved in classes and finding new interests. Camilla tried activities like painting, yoga and even rock climbing. The community center helped Camilla find new interests and hobbies.

Part A: Check Each Box as you Complete the Task

❑   **Read the Story**
❑   **Circle the word** (interests) **in the story**
❑   **Trace & Write the word below:**

___interests___   _____

Part B: Fill in the Blank

1. **Who is this story about?**

   _____

2. **What are some of Camilla's new interests?**

   _____

3. **When did her opinion of the community center change?**

   _____

Part C: Write the Main Idea of the Story

_____

_____

_____

_____

_____

Part D: Write One Supporting Detail from the Story

_____

_____

_____

_____

_____

Part E: Do you think that Camilia changing her attitude had an impact on how much she enjoyed the community center outings with her class?

_____

_____

_____

_____

_____

_____

_____

_____

_____

_____

Community Center: Interests

A good way to make new friends is to share interests. When you first meet someone, it is a good idea to ask them what they are interested in. Lillian met a new friend named Jeremiah at the community center. Jeremiah said he was interested in weight training.

Lillian had never learned much about exercising with weights before but, after talking to Jeremiah she decided she wanted to know more. Lillian signed up for a weight training class and read as many books about it as she could. She became an expert! Lillian now shares her interest in weight training with the new friends she meets.

Part A: Check Each Box as you Complete the Task

☐   **Read the Story**
☐   **Circle the word interests in the story**
☐   **Trace & Write the word below:**

interests _____ _____

Part B: Fill in the Blank

1. **Who is this story about?**

   _____

2. **Who introduced Lillian to weight training?**

   _____

3. **How is Lillian becoming an expert in weight training?**

   _____

Part C: Write the Main Idea of the Story

_____

_____

_____

_____

_____

Part D: Write One Supporting Detail from the Story

_____

_____

_____

_____

_____

Part E: How can meeting new people lead you to having new interests?

_____

_____

_____

_____

_____

_____

_____

_____

_____

Exploring your interests can be a fun way to spend time in your community. Make a list of things you are interested in learning more about.

_____

_____

_____

_____

_____

_____

_____

_____

_____

_____

_____

_____

My sketch of one thing I am interested in learning more about:

Community Center: Events

Being willing to try something new is a personal goal for Sadie. Sadie likes to stick with what she knows. New things make her feel uncomfortable. Her teacher has reminded Sadie that she might find something she loves if she is willing to try new things.

So Sadie is going to a camping skills event at her local community center. The event is four hours long and will teach Sadie how to build a fire, set up a tent, and look for wildlife. Sadie is nervous but also very excited to try this new event.

Part A: Check Each Box as you Complete the Task

❑   **Read the Story**
❑   **Circle the word (event) in the story**
❑   **Trace & Write the word below:**

event

-----------------------------   -----------------------------

Part B: Fill in the Blank

1. Who is this story about?

_____

2. How does Sadie feel about trying new things?

_____

3. Where is the camping skills event being held?

_____

Part C: Write the Main Idea of the Story

_____

_____

_____

_____

_____

Part D: Write One Supporting Detail from the Story

_____

_____

_____

_____

_____

Part E: Do you think it is important to attend events and learn about new things even if it makes you feel uncomfortable? Why or why not?

_____

_____

_____

_____

_____

_____

_____

_____

_____

Community Center: Events

A community center is a good place to find out about new events. Caleb read the list of events that were posted on the back wall. He hoped that he would find something that interested him.

He read about craft fairs, bowling tournaments, reading clubs and a three-day karate workshop! Caleb asked questions about the karate workshop that was coming in fall. He found out that it was a perfect match for him. Caleb signed up for the workshop. He had always wanted to learn about karate and now he had his chance thanks to the community center.

Part A: Check Each Box as you Complete the Task

❑   Read the Story
❑   Circle the word (events) in the story
❑   Trace & Write the word below:

events

_____   _____

Part B: Fill in the Blank

1. Who is this story about?

    _____

2. What kind of event is Caleb interested in attending?

    _____

3. When is the karate workshop?

    _____

Part C: Write the Main Idea of the Story

_____

_____

_____

_____

_____

Part D: Write One Supporting Detail from the Story

_____

_____

_____

_____

_____

Part E: Deepen your Understanding

What types of events is Caleb most interested in?

a. Craft Fairs

b. Karate Workshops

c. Bowling Tournaments

D. Reading Clubs

How long is the karate workshop?

a. 2 hours

b. 6 months

c. 3 days

D. 3 hours

How can you learn about events that are happening in your community?

_____

_____

_____

_____

_____

_____

_____

_____

_____

_____

_____

_____

_____

My sketch of an event in my community:

Community Center Skills

- ☐ Exercise
- ☐ Participate in Activities
- ☐ Make Connections
- ☐ Explore Interests
- ☐ Learn about Events

Here is what I know about community centers:

My favorite thing to do at a community center:

One community center skill I am already good at is...

Make a Connection

Some interests I would like to explore at the community center are:

○

○

○

○

○

○

○

○

○

○

I will need to practice these skills to be successful at a community center...

Think about your community center outing. How did you do?

Rate yourself on each skill you practiced while you were there.

SKILL	5 Points	3 Points	1 Point
Exercise	○ Participated willingly in individual or group exercise ○ Stretched out before & after ○ Drank water	○ Unwillingly participated in individual or group exercise ○ Stretched out before or after ○ Drank water with prompts from an adult	○ Did not participate in exercise ○ Did not drink water
Participation	○ Made an effort to get involved ○ Played a game, sport or took a class ○ Positive attitude ○ Open body language	○ Made an effort to get involved with adult prompts ○ Played a game, sport or took a class when invited ○ Mostly positive attitude ○ Mostly open body language	○ Made no effort to get involved ○ Did not play a game, sport or take a class ○ Negative attitude ○ Closed body language
Connection	○ Reviewed list of activities to find a group or class of interest ○ Sought out peers to collaborate on activities ○ Engaged with new peers	○ Reviewed list of activities with help from an adult ○ Collaborated on activities ○ Responded to new peers	○ Did not investigate new activities ○ Played/worked alone ○ Did not respond to new peers
Interests	○ Started conversations about things I find interesting ○ Started conversations about things others find interesting ○ Asked questions about other's interests	○ Participated in conversations about things I find interesting ○ Responded to questions about my interests	○ Did not participate in conversations about interests ○ Did not ask questions or respond to other's questions
Events	○ Asked questions about upcoming events ○ Made a plan to attend an upcoming event ○ Willing to try new activity	○ Read about upcoming events ○ Showed an interest in attending events ○ Willing to try new activity with adult support	○ Did not show an interest in attending events ○ Unwilling to try new activity

Student Name:

Today, I feel I earned

Total Points: /25

Looking at my rubric I see...

It is
important
to get involved
in my
community
center
because...

I am proud of:

_____
_____
_____
_____
_____
_____
_____
_____

I need to keep working on:

_____
_____
_____
_____
_____
_____

Community Based Instruction

Public Transportation

Find the Bus Stop

Get On the Correct Bus

Pay or Use a Bus Pass

Ride the Bus Safely

Get Off the Bus Appropriately

Community Based Instruction

Warm Up:
Public Transportation

Something I **enjoy** about using public transportation... ⬇

One type of public transportation I have taken... ➡

Something I **do not** enjoy about using public transportation:

⬇

Here are a few **skills** I think people need to have to use public transportation:

Public Transportation: Find the Bus Stop

Isaiah wanted to go to the new game store that opened close to his house. His parents told him he would need to take the bus. Isaiah got online and researched where the closest bus stop was.

He found that he needed to take bus 36 and that the bus stop was just three blocks from his house. Isaiah used the bus route schedule he found on the back of his bus map and discovered that the bus would arrive at 2:30pm. Isaiah was excited because he knew he would be able to take the 2:30pm bus right after school and return on the 4:10pm bus. He already knew which game he wanted to buy. Isaiah was thankful that there was a bus to get him to the game store!

Part A: Check Each Box as you Complete the Task

❑ **Read the Story**
❑ **Circle the words** bus stop **in the story**
❑ **Trace & Write the word below:**

_____ bus stop _____   _____

Part B: Fill in the Blank

1. **Who is this story about?**

   _____

2. **Where does Isaiah want to go?**

   _____

3. **How will Isaiah get there?**

   _____

Part C: Write the Main Idea of the Story

_____

_____

_____

_____

_____

Part D: Write One Supporting Detail from the Story

_____

_____

_____

_____

_____

Part E: Deepen your Understanding

How did Isaiah know where the bus stop was located?

a. He asked a friend

b. He called the video game store

c. He looked online

d. He walked around until he found it

What does Isaiah want to buy?

a. A game

b. A sweatshirt

c. A pizza

d. A new cell phone

Public Transportation: Find the Bus Stop

When Victoria got to the bus to stop to go to her work, she was right on time. The bus, was not. She could not believe it. Victoria worried that she would be late for work and that her boss would be disappointed.

Victoria worked at the front desk in a medical office and people were depending on her. She took a deep breath and waited patiently. Once the bus arrived Victoria was friendly to the driver because she knew that being rude would not help anything.

She found her seat quickly so the bus would get on the road as soon as possible. Then, Victoria called her office to let them know that the bus was running a few minutes late.

Part A: Check Each Box as you Complete the Task

❑   Read the Story
❑   Circle the words ⟨bus stop⟩ in the story
❑   Trace & Write the word below:

_bus stop_____   _____

Part B: Fill in the Blank

1. Who is this story about?

    _____

2. What was Victoria worried about?

    _____

3. Where does Victoria work?

    _____

Part C: Write the Main Idea of the Story

_____
_____
_____
_____
_____

Part D: Write One Supporting Detail from the Story

_____
_____
_____
_____
_____

Part E: How do you think Victoria's boss responded when Victoria called to say the bus was running late?

_____
_____
_____
_____
_____
_____
_____
_____
_____

List two ways you can find out where the closest bus stops are to your home.

_____

_____

_____

_____

_____

_____

_____

_____

_____

_____

_____

_____

My sketch of one type of public transportation:

Public Transportation: Get on the Bus

Olivia was getting ready to take the bus for the first time by herself. She had a dentist appointment that was on the other side of town from where she lived. Olivia was a little nervous because she had to change busses. She used the bus route map to make a plan.

She planned to take bus 22 to the red stop and then transfer to bus 10. That way, the bus would stop right in front of her dentist's office and should could get off without having to walk far. Olivia found the bus stop she needed and was sure to go a few minutes early so she could get there on time and without having to rush.

Part A: Check Each Box as you Complete the Task

- ❏ **Read the Story**
- ❏ **Circle the word** (bus) **in the story**
- ❏ **Trace & Write the word below:**

bus
------------------------   ------------------------

Part B: Fill in the Blank

1. **Who is this story about?**

   _____

2. **Where is Olivia going?**

   _____

3. **Why is Olivia nervous?**

   _____

Part C: Write the Main Idea of the Story

_____

_____

_____

_____

_____

Part D: Write One Supporting Detail from the Story

_____

_____

_____

_____

_____

Part E: Deepen your Understanding

Circle all of the busses Olivia will take to the dentist office.	How did Olivia know which busses to take?
a. 22	a. She remembered
b. 26	b. She asked her teacher
c. 10	c. She looked online
D. 4	D. She used the bus route map

Public Transportation: Get on the Bus

When Nathan gets to the bus stop he is surprised. Normally, he's able to walk onto the bus with no waiting. But today, there's a soccer game at the coliseum and the bus stop is filled with soccer fans wearing the green and yellow Portland Timbers Soccer colors. It's raining and Nathan is annoyed that his cozy bus stop has been invaded.

He pushes his way to the front of the line and gets mean looks from some of the people waiting. Nathan crosses his arms and sighs loudly. The people around him give him weird looks and feel uncomfortable. He knows that he is waiting impatiently. It does not make Nathan or anyone around him feel good. Next time, Nathan will try to get on the bus with a better attitude.

Part A: Check Each Box as you Complete the Task

❑ **Read the Story**
❑ **Circle the word (bus) in the story**
❑ **Trace & Write the word below:**

bus

_____   _____

Part B: Fill in the Blank

1. **Who is the story about?**

_____

2. **Why is Nathan feeling surprised?**

_____

3. **Do you think Nathan was happy about the surprise?**

_____

Part C: Write the Main Idea of the Story

_____

_____

_____

_____

_____

Part D: Write One Supporting Detail from the Story

_____

_____

_____

_____

_____

Part E: What could Nathan have done differently to get on the bus in a polite way?

_____

_____

_____

_____

_____

_____

_____

_____

What does it look like to get onto a city bus in a polite way?

_____

_____

_____

_____

_____

_____

_____

_____

_____

_____

_____

My sketch of an overcrowded bus stop:

Public Transportation: Pay or Use a Bus Pass

Logan was going to take the bus to his favorite used book store. He loved the comics they sold there! Before he left the house, he took out all of his money and organized it. He made sure that he had the correct change to pay the bus fare.

Logan put his bus money in his front pocket so it was ready to go. This included the money he would need to pay for his return trip. Logan kept the money he would use to pay for the comics separately in his wallet.

Part A: Check Each Box as you Complete the Task

☐ Read the Story
☐ Circle the word (pay) in the story
☐ Trace & Write the word below:

_____pay_____   _____

Part B: Fill in the Blank

1. Who is the story about?

   _____

2. Where is he going?

   _____

3. Where does Logan keep his bus money?

   _____

Public Transportation: Pay or Use Bus Pass

Part C: Write the Main Idea of the Story

_____

_____

_____

_____

Part D: Write One Supporting Detail from the Story

_____

_____

_____

_____

Part E Do you think it is a good idea for Logan to keep his bus money separate from his spending money? Why or why not?

_____

_____

_____

_____

_____

_____

_____

Public Transportation: Pay or Use a Bus Pass

Hannah uses her bus pass to pay for her bus ride on the city bus during her class trips to the community center. When she gets to the community center, she participates in a swimming class.

Hannah's bus pass allows her to take as many trips as she wants without having to pay each time. Since she needs to scan her bus pass every time she uses it, Hannah is sure to keep it in a safe place. She does not want to lose the pass because it is as valuable as money. Every single time she is done using her bus pass, Hannah puts it back into a special place in her wallet.

Part A: Check Each Box as you Complete the Task

❑ Read the Story
❑ Circle the words bus pass in the story
❑ Trace & Write the word below:

bus pass _____

Part B: Fill in the Blank

1. Who is the story about?

_____

2. Where is Hannah's class going on the city bus?

_____

3. Where does Hannah keep her bus pass?

_____

Public Transportation: Pay or Use Bus Pass

Part C: Write the Main Idea of the Story

_____

_____

_____

_____

_____

Part D: Write One Supporting Detail from the Story

_____

_____

_____

_____

_____

Part E Why does Hannah think that her bus pass is as valuable as money?

_____

_____

_____

_____

_____

_____

_____

_____

Why should a bus pass be treated like it is as valuable as money? Where should you keep a bus pass?

_____

_____

_____

_____

_____

_____

_____

_____

_____

_____

_____

_____

_____

My sketch of a bus route map:

Public Transportation: Ride the Bus Safely

Ezra is taking the bus today with his class for an outing to Paul's Pizza. Ezra has worked with his teacher to set a goal of riding the bus safely. This means, when the bus doors open, he will walk calmly onto the bus. Ezra will look for the closest open seat. He will sit down quickly and keep his belongings to himself. He has his coat, laptop computer and backpack with him.

Ezra entering the bus safely will help the bus stay on schedule and will allow everyone to get on as quickly as possible. While the bus is driving, Ezra will stay seated and watch for his stop. Ezra will meet his goal of riding the bus safely.

Part A: Check Each Box as you Complete the Task

❑   Read the Story
❑   Circle the words ⟨bus pass⟩ in the story
❑   Trace & Write the word below:

_____bus pass_____   _____

Part B: Fill in the Blank

1. Who is the story about?

   _____

2. Where is Ezra going?

   _____

3. What does Ezra do to stay safe while he is on the bus?

   _____

Public Transportation: Ride the Bus Safely

Part C: Write the Main Idea of the Story

_____

_____

_____

_____

_____

Part D: Write One Supporting Detail from the Story

_____

_____

_____

_____

_____

Part E: Deepen your Understanding

Which item does Ezra not bring with him on the bus?

a. Hat

b. Coat

c. Backpack

d. Laptop Computer

What might happen if Ezra stood up while the bus was moving?

_____

_____

_____

_____

_____

_____

_____

_____

_____

Public Transportation: Ride the Bus Safely

Elena is riding the bus with her younger brother. They are going to the grocery store to buy butter. They want to surprise their dad by making a cake for him on his birthday.

Elena wants to get there quickly and safely. She and her brother will stay together and keep their grocery bags with them. Elena knows it is important to stay aware when riding the bus. She does not look at her phone or listen to music. This way she can pay attention and look for their stop. Elena keeps her brother safe by making sure he is sitting while the bus is moving.

Part A: Check Each Box as you Complete the Task

❑   Read the Story
❑   Circle the words (safe) in the story
❑   Trace & Write the word below:

safe

_____   _____

Part B: Fill in the Blank

1. Who is the story about?

_____

2. What does Elena do to stay safe while riding the bus?

_____

_____

_____

Public Transportation: Ride the Bus Safely

Part C: Write the Main Idea of the Story

_____

_____

_____

_____

_____

Part D: Write One Supporting Detail from the Story

_____

_____

_____

_____

_____

Part E: Deepen your Understanding

Which of these is not something Elena does to stay safe while riding the bus?

a. Sits quickly with her brother

b. Reads a book

c. Keeps her belongings close

d. Pays attention to her surroundings

What is Elena buying at the store?

a. Butter

b. Flour

c. A cake

d. Vegetables

List three things you can do to ride a bus safely.

_____

_____

_____

_____

_____

_____

_____

_____

_____

_____

_____

_____

My sketch of myself safely boarding a bus:

Public Transportation: Get Off the Bus

Isaac took some of his dirty clothes to the laundry mat. It's only a few stops down from his house. He looked out of the window as the bus drove. When he saw the laundry mat in the distance he pulled the "stop requested cord" to alert the driver that he wanted to get off.

This gave the driver enough time to stop right in front of the laundry mat. It takes a while to for the bus to stop because the bus driver waits until it is safe. Isaac stayed seated while he waited for the bus to stop. He made sure he gathered all of his belongings. When it was completely still, he stood and walked calmly to the door to exit. Isaac did not have to walk far with his bag of laundry.

Part A: Check Each Box as you Complete the Task

❑   **Read the Story**
❑   **Circle the word (stop) in the story**
❑   **Trace & Write the word below:**

stop

_____   _____

Part B: Fill in the Blank

1. **Who is the story about?**

   _____

2. **Where is Isaac going?**

   _____

3. **When does he pull the "stop requested cord"?**

   _____

Public Transportation: Get Off the Bus

Part C: Write the Main Idea of the Story

_____

_____

_____

_____

_____

Part D: Write One Supporting Detail from the Story

_____

_____

_____

_____

_____

Part E: List three things Isaac does that help him get off of the bus safely.

_____

_____

_____

_____

_____

_____

_____

_____

Public Transportation: Get Off the Bus

Aaliyah was heading home on the city bus from her office. Aaliyah knew that her bus stop was coming up quickly. She had so many things with her; flowers from the market, her work purse, and a bag of groceries.

Aaliyah knew it would take her a few minutes to collect her things. So, as soon as the bus turned into her neighborhood, Aaliyah gathered her belongings. When the bus stopped in front of her house she was able to stand quickly and get off of the bus. She knew that she did not leave anything behind because she double checked. Aaliyah got off of the bus safely and appropriately.

Part A: Check Each Box as you Complete the Task

❑   **Read the Story**
❑   **Circle the word (off) in the story**
❑   **Trace & Write the word below:**

off

-------------------------   -------------------------

Part B: Fill in the Blank

1. **Who is the story about?**

_____

2. **When does Aaliyah start collecting her belongings to get off of the bus?**

_____

_____

Part C: Write the Main Idea of the Story

_____

_____

_____

_____

_____

Part D: Write One Supporting Detail from the Story

_____

_____

_____

_____

_____

Part E: Deepen your Understanding

What does Aaliyah <u>not</u> have with her?

a. Flowers from the market

b. Pink umbrella

c. Her work purse

d. Groceries

Where was she coming from?

a. The grocery store

b. Her office

c. Her parents house

d. School

What does it look like to get off of a bus appropriately?

_____

_____

_____

_____

_____

_____

_____

_____

_____

_____

_____

_____

_____

My sketch of what it looks like to wait for the bus patiently:

109

Public Transportation Skills

Check point! Review each skill.

- ☐ Find the Bus Stop
- ☐ Get on the Correct Bus
- ☐ Pay or Use a Bus Pass
- ☐ Ride the Bus Safely
- ☐ Get Off the Bus

Here is what I know about public transportation:

My favorite type of transportation:

One public transportation skill I am already good at is...

Public Transportation Skills I need to Practice are:

○

○

○

○

○

○

○

○

○

One place I would like to go using public transportation is...

The type of public transportation available near my home is...

Think about your outing on public transportation. How did you do?

Rate yourself on each skill you practiced while you were there.

Date:

Destination:

SKILL	5 Points	3 Points	1 Point
Found the Bus Stop	○ Researched where the bus stops prior to leaving ○ Walked on sidewalks ○ Crossed the street using crosswalks	○ Worked with an adult or map to find the bus stop ○ Walked on sidewalks with reminders ○ Crossed the street safely	○ Followed an adult to the bus stop ○ Walked in the street ○ Crossed streets unsafely
Got on the Correct Bus	○ Arrived a few minutes early ○ Read the routes map to find which bus to get on ○ Waited patiently ○ Waited safely out of the street	○ Arrived on time ○ Asked an adult which bus to get on ○ Waited ○ Stayed out of the street with adult support	○ Missed the bus ○ Was unsure of which bus to get on ○ Impatient ○ Stood/walked into the street
Paid or Used my Bus Pass	○ Had money or pass organized, out & ready ○ Put pass or change safely back into wallet ○ Friendly to the driver	○ Had money or pass ○ Took pass or change ○ Made eye contact with the driver	○ Forgot money or pass ○ Did not take change or pass after boarding ○ Unfriendly to the driver
Rode the Bus Safely	○ Walked onto the bus ○ Found a seat quickly or stood holding on ○ Kept my belongings safely with me ○ Stayed aware of my surroundings	○ Walked quickly onto the bus ○ Searched for the perfect seat or stood leaning against pole ○ Put my belongings on a seat near me ○ Looked around every once in a while	○ Ran, hopped or leapt onto the bus ○ Passed many open seats or stood without holding on ○ Put my belongings on the floor
Got Off of the Bus Appropriately	○ Pulled the stop request cord right before my stop ○ Gathered my belongings ahead of time ○ Walked to the door	○ Pulled the stop request cord when we passed my stop ○ Gathered my belongings after we stopped ○ Walked fast to the door	○ Did not pull the stop request cord ○ Left my belongings ○ Ran, hopped, or jumped to the door

Student Name:

Today, I feel I earned

Total Points: ____ /25

Looking at my rubric I see...

_____

_____

_____

_____

_____

It is important to learn how to use public transportation because...

I am proud of:

_____

_____

_____

_____

_____

_____

_____

I need to keep working on:

_____

_____

_____

_____

_____

_____

_____

Community Based Instruction

Library **Skills**

Find Books of Interest

Use the Computers

Follow the Rules

Check Out a Book

Learn about Events

Warm Up: Library

My community library has... →

Something I enjoy about going to the library...

Something I do not enjoy about going to the library...

Here are a few skills I think people need to have to go to a library:

Library Skill: Find Books of Interest

Emma is with her class on an outing to the library. She is so excited because she loves books. The problem is, she can never find the types of books she likes until library time is almost over.

Today her goal is to locate books of interest right away. Emma will use the computer system to type in a few books that she has already researched online. It should be easy because she has made a list of book titles along with the author's name. This will help Emma quickly find books that she may want to read or borrow from the library.

Part A: Check Each Box as you Complete the Task

❑   **Read the Story**
❑   **Circle the word (books) in the story**
❑   **Trace & Write the word below:**

books

------------------------------   ------------------------------

Part B: Fill in the Blank

1. Who is the story about?

_____

2. Why is Emma excited to go to the library?

_____

3. How will Emma find the books she is interested in?

_____

Library Skills: Find Books of Interest

Part C: Write the Main Idea of the Story

_____

_____

_____

_____

_____

Part D: Write One Supporting Detail from the Story

_____

_____

_____

_____

_____

Part E: Deepen your Understanding

How did Emma come up with her list of books she is interested in?

a. Asked her friends

b. Searched online

c. Watched a YouTube video

d. Asked her parents

What information did Emma write down about the books she is interested in?

a. The author and number of pages

b. The author and the illustrator

c. The author and the title

d. Only the title

Library Skill: Find Books of Interest

James likes to read but is not always sure of which books he wants to choose at the library. Before he goes to the library James looks online for book recommendations.

He starts by searching for topics that he is interested in like video games and airplanes. James looks on blogs and asks his friends if they have read anything interesting lately. Then, he asks his teacher for her recommendations because she is an expert in books!

By the time his class gets ready to leave the school, James has a list of four book topics he will search for as soon as he gets to the library.

Part A: Check Each Box as you Complete the Task

❑   Read the Story
❑   Circle the word books in the story
❑   Trace & Write the word below:

_____books_____   _____

Part B: Fill in the Blank

1. Who is the story about?

_____

2. Where does James start when looking for books?

_____

3. What does James ask his teacher for?

_____

Part C: Write the Main Idea of the Story

_____

_____

_____

_____

_____

Part D: Write One Supporting Detail from the Story

_____

_____

_____

_____

Part E: Deepen your Understanding

Which of these are James' interests?

a. Video games and soccer

b. Crafting and basketball

c. Airplanes and art

d. Airplanes and video games

Which of these is <u>not</u> a way James finds interesting books?

a. Blogs
b. Recommendations from friends
c. Recommendations from the librarian
d. Recommendations from his teacher

What are some ways you can find recommendations for books that are interesting to you?

_____

_____

_____

_____

_____

_____

_____

_____

_____

_____

_____

_____

_____

My sketch of my favorite books:

Library Skill: Use the Computer

Mia is excited because her parents are taking her to the library. She is looking forward to using the computers. She will look for new recipes to try with the apples she collected from the orchard behind her grandparents house.

Mia knows that she will need her library card to use the computers. She is sure to bring it with her. When Mia finds a recipe for warm apple crumble she knows she has found the one she wants to make! She prints the recipe and grabs the paper off of the printer. Mia shows her parents. They head home and get all of their ingredients together.

Part A: Check Each Box as you Complete the Task

❑   **Read the Story**
❑   **Circle the word** computers **in the story**
❑   **Trace & Write the word below:**

computers   _____

Part B: Fill in the Blank

1. **Who is the story about?**

_____

2. **What is Mia printing from the library computers?**

_____

3. **Where did Mia get her apples?**

_____

Part C: Write the Main Idea of the Story

_____

_____

_____

_____

_____

Part D: Write One Supporting Detail from the Story

_____

_____

_____

_____

_____

Part E Why do you think Mia needs her library card to print from the library computers?

_____

_____

_____

_____

_____

_____

_____

_____

_____

Library Skill: Use the Computer

Today Samuel was at the library searching for science fair project ideas. When he found a project about volcanoes, he knew that was the one for him! Samuel dashed away from his computer to tell his teacher that he had chosen a project.

He is disappointed in himself because he forgot to log off of the computer when he was done. Samuel worried that another person might sit down and use his internet time. At Samuel's library, you only get two hours of library time each day. They keep track of your time by using your library card number. It is important to log out of the computers when you are done.

Part A: Check Each Box as you Complete the Task

☐   **Read the Story**
☐   **Circle the word** computers **in the story**
☐   **Trace & Write the word below:**

computers   _____

Part B: Fill in the Blank

1. **Who is the story about?**

_____

2. **What is Samuel searching for on the library computer?**

_____

3. **Why is Samuel disappointed in himself?**

_____

<u>Part C:</u> Write the Main Idea of the Story

_____

_____

_____

_____

_____

<u>Part D:</u> Write One Supporting Detail from the Story

_____

_____

_____

_____

_____

<u>Part E:</u> Deepen your Understanding

How much computer time does Samuel's library card get him each day?

a. 1 hour

b. 2 hours

c. 3 hours

d. Unlimited hours

How does the library keep track of computer time?

a. By last name

b. By topic researched

c. By school attended

d. By library card number

How can the computers at the library help you find a book that is interesting to you?

_____

_____

_____

_____

_____

_____

_____

_____

_____

_____

_____

_____

My sketch of the library closest to my house:

Library Skill: Follow the Rules

When Dominic arrived at the library on his outing with his class, he had one goal; to follow the rules. Last time his class went to the library, Dominic was so excited he ran through the library doors and shouted at his friends. He disrupted the people who were already at the library.

Dominic knows that the library is a place people go to study, work, and read in peace. Respecting the library rules allows everyone enjoy the library. Today, Dominic will work on his goal by walking in quietly and calmly. He will also be sure to give his classmates personal space so they can have the time to work.

Part A: Check Each Box as you Complete the Task

❑   Read the Story
❑   Circle the word (rules) in the story
❑   Trace & Write the word below:

rules
_____   _____

Part B: Fill in the Blank

1. Who is the story about?

_____

2. Where is Dominic going on his outing with his class?

_____

3. What is Dominic's goal for the outing?

_____

Part C: Write the Main Idea of the Story

_____

_____

_____

_____

_____

Part D: Write One Supporting Detail from the Story

_____

_____

_____

_____

_____

Part E Why is it important to give others personal space at the library?

_____

_____

_____

_____

_____

_____

_____

_____

Library Skill: Follow the Rules

Chloe decided that she was going to check out two books at the library. When she found her favorite section with books about mermaids, dragons and dinosaurs, she sat down comfortably on the floor. Chloe pulled out thirteen books and read the back cover of each book. She narrowed the books down according to which books had the most magic in it. When she finally made a decision about the two books she wanted to borrow, she had a pile of eleven books she needed to reshelf. It is important to reshelf books in the correct locations because it allows other people to find them. Chloe took her time and put each book back in its correct location. There were a few she was unsure of so she left those on a reshelf cart for the librarian.

Part A: Check Each Box as you Complete the Task

❑   Read the Story
❑   Circle the word (rules) in the story
❑   Trace & Write the word below:

rules   _____

Part B: Fill in the Blank

1. Who is the story about?

_____

2. What does it mean to "reshelf" a book?

_____

3. Why is it important to reshelf a book?

_____

Part C: Write the Main Idea of the Story

_____

_____

_____

_____

_____

Part D: Write One Supporting Detail from the Story

_____

_____

_____

_____

_____

Part E: Deepen your Understanding

How many books did Chloe check out?

    a. 13

    b. 11

    c. 2

    d. 8

Which of these is not a topic that Chloe wants to read about?

    a. Mermaids

    b. Historical figures

    c. Dinosaurs

    D. Dragons

Make a list of rules you think all people should follow when they are at a library.

_____

_____

_____

_____

_____

_____

_____

_____

_____

_____

_____

_____

_____

My sketch of a messy bookshelf:

133

Library Skill: Check Out a Book

When Julian goes to the school library with his class today, he wants to pick out a book on his own. His teacher, Mr. Righty usually chooses books for them. But, today it is Julian's goal to do it on his own.

Mr. Righty told Julian that he can pick a book on his own if he follows two rules. First, the book must be interesting to him. Second, it must be written at a good reading level for him, not too hard and not too easy.

Julian knows that he will be able to find a book that does both! As soon as they reach the library, Julian heads toward his favorite section, the joke books.

Part A: Check Each Box as you Complete the Task

❑   **Read the Story**
❑   **Circle the words check out in the story**
❑   **Trace & Write the word below:**

check out   _____

Part B: Fill in the Blank

1. **Who is the story about?**

_____

2. **What is Julian excited about?**

_____

3. **Who usually picks out the books Julian checks out?**

_____

Part C: Write the Main Idea of the Story

_____

_____

_____

_____

_____

Part D: Write One Supporting Detail from the Story

_____

_____

_____

_____

Part E What are the two rules Julian must follow when picking out his library books?

_____

_____

_____

_____

_____

_____

_____

_____

_____

Library Skill: Check Out a Book

Lily signed up for her very own library card. She is excited! With her new library card, Lily is able to check out books, borrow movies, and listen to music. She is allowed to use the computers for free and print the things she needs for school.

She never lets anyone borrow her library card and she keeps it in a safe location in her wallet. When Lily borrows books by checking them out, she is sure to keep them safe and clean. She always returns them on time. Lily knows that having a library card is a big responsibility and she is taking it seriously.

Part A: Check Each Box as you Complete the Task

❑   **Read the Story**
❑   **Circle the words** (check out) **in the story**
❑   **Trace & Write the word below:**

check out _____   _____

Part B: Fill in the Blank

1. Who is the story about?

_____

2. What can Lily do with her new library card?

_____

_____

Part C: Write the Main Idea of the Story

_____

_____

_____

_____

_____

Part D: Write One Supporting Detail from the Story

_____

_____

_____

_____

_____

Part E: Deepen your Understanding

What can Lily not check out with her library card?	How can Lily take care of her borrowed books?
a. Books	
b. Movies	
c. Cell phones	
d. Music	

List five ways you can take care of the books you borrow from the library.

_____

_____

_____

_____

_____

_____

_____

_____

_____

_____

_____

_____

138

My sketch of one thing you can do with a library card:

Library Skill: Community Events

Luke is on an outing to the community library with his class. When they walk in the door, he notices a board with a calendar on it. The calendar shows all of the upcoming events at the library for the month. One of the events said "Book Talk" and to Luke's surprise it was with his favorite author L.L. Ward. He could hardly believe it!

Luke took a picture of the calendar with his phone. He would be sure to ask his parents to bring him back to the library to meet his favorite author in person. Luke was excited to hear the author read, talk about books and to have his book signed.

Part A: Check Each Box as you Complete the Task

❑   Read the Story
❑   Circle the word ⟨events⟩ in the story
❑   Trace & Write the word below:

events _____

Part B: Fill in the Blank

1. Who is the story about?

_____

2. Who is Luke's favorite author?

_____

3. What type of event is Luke looking forward to?

_____

Part C: Write the Main Idea of the Story

_____

_____

_____

_____

_____

Part D: Write One Supporting Detail from the Story

_____

_____

_____

_____

_____

Part E What do you think the "Book Talk" might be like?

_____

_____

_____

_____

_____

_____

_____

_____

_____

Library Skill: Community Events

At the community library Sophia noticed a sign up form for a newsletter that is emailed out each month. She signed up right away! Sophia lived close enough to the library to walk with her parents and she loved attending library events.

She always looked forward to the emails and read them right away. Sophia saw an event in the September email that said "crafts." She loved painting, pottery, and scrapbooking so she was excited to attend. Receiving emails about community library events gave Sophia and her parents something to look forward to doing together each month!

Part A: Check Each Box as you Complete the Task

❑   **Read the Story**
❑   **Circle the word** events **in the story**
❑   **Trace & Write the word below:**

events _____   _____

Part B: Fill in the Blank

1. **Who is the story about?**

_____

2. **How does Sophia get to the library for events?**

_____

3. **How does Sophia know what events are happening?**

_____

Part C: Write the Main Idea of the Story

_____

_____

_____

_____

_____

Part D: Write One Supporting Detail from the Story

_____

_____

_____

_____

Part E What type of event would you like to attend at a library?

_____

_____

_____

_____

_____

_____

_____

_____

_____

What types of community events do they offer at your community library?

_____

_____

_____

_____

_____

_____

_____

_____

_____

_____

_____

_____

_____

My sketch of a "Book Talk" with my favorite author:

Library Skills

Check point! Review each skill.

- ☐ Find Books of Interest
- ☐ Use the Computers
- ☐ Follow the Library Rules
- ☐ Check Out a Book
- ☐ Learn about Community Events

Here is what I know about libraries:

My favorite thing to do at the library:

One library skill I am already good at is...

Make a Connection

Library Skills I need to Practice are:

○

○

○

○

○

○

○

My favorite kind of book to read is...

Something I like about the library in my town is...

Think about your library outing. How did you do?

Rate yourself on each skill you practiced while you were there.

Library: Self Assessment

Date:

Library Name:

SKILL	5 Points	3 Points	1 Point
Found Books of Interest	○ Used computer system to locate a specific genre ○ Had 2 or more books or topics of interest in mind ○ Searched by author or title for specific books	○ Asked librarian to locate a genre ○ Had a book or topic of interest in mind ○ Searched for a specific type book	○ Looked randomly for books ○ Had no books or topics of interest in mind ○ Did not find an interesting book
Used the Computers	○ Used library card to login independently ○ Accessed a specified website independently ○ Printed documents independently ○ Logged off independently	○ Used library card to login with support ○ Accessed a specified website with support ○ Printed documents with support ○ Logged off with a prompt from an adult	○ Unable to login ○ Attempted to access inappropriate content ○ Unable to print documents ○ Logged off with resistance or multiple prompts
Followed the Library Rules	○ Quiet voice ○ Reshelf books in the correct locations ○ Walked ○ Respected others personal space	○ Mostly quiet voice ○ Put books back on shelves in random locations ○ Walked quickly ○ Mostly respected others personal space	○ Loud voice ○ Did not put books back on shelves ○ Ran, hopped or jumped ○ Invaded others personal space
Checked Out a Book	○ Selected a high interested book ○ Selected a book with a reading level that was a good fit for me ○ Used my library card independently	○ Selected a high interest book with support ○ Selected a book with a reading level that was almost a good fit for me ○ Used my library card with support	○ Did not choose a book I am interested in ○ Selected a book with a too difficult or too simple reading level for me ○ Forgot or did not use my library card
Learned about Community Events	○ Read about upcoming community events ○ Selected one that I would like to attend ○ Asked questions to the library staff about events	○ Found upcoming community events listings ○ Considered whether or not I would like to attend any of them with prompts from an adult	○ Did not locate the events listings ○ Uninterested in community events

Student Name:

Today, I feel I earned

Total Points: _____ /25

Looking at my rubric I see...

It is important to know how to use the library because...

I am proud of:

_____

_____

_____

_____

_____

_____

_____

I need to keep working on:

_____

_____

_____

_____

_____

_____

_____

Community Based Instruction

Shopping

Skills

Use a List

Compare Prices

Stay within budget

Shop Politely

Pay for your Items

Community Based Instruction

Warm Up: Shopping

One store I have been to...

Why do you need to learn skills to go shopping on your own?

Something I do not enjoy about going shopping...

My favorite thing to shop for...

Here are a few skills I think people need to have to go shopping:

Shopping Skill: Use a List

Maya knows that her class is going on an outing to the store today. She wants to make sure she gets everything they need to make their class lunches for the week. So, Maya makes a list.

She sits down with her teacher and writes each ingredient they need to make sandwiches including; bread, turkey, cheese, and mustard. Maya folds the list and sticks it into her front pocket.

Using a list will help Maya stay within her budget since she will not buy extra items. She will use her list at the store to be sure she buys exactly what her class needs.

Part A: Check Each Box as you Complete the Task

☐ Read the Story
☐ Circle the word (list) in the story
☐ Trace & Write the word below:

list

--------------------------   --------------------------

Part B: Fill in the Blank

1. Who is the story about?

_____

2. Where is Maya's class going on their outing today?

_____

3. Where does Maya keep her list?

_____

Part C: Write the Main Idea of the Story

_____

_____

_____

_____

_____

Part D: Write One Supporting Detail from the Story

_____

_____

_____

_____

_____

Part E How will having a list help Maya stay within her budget?

_____

_____

_____

_____

_____

_____

_____

_____

_____

Shopping Skill: Use a List

When Theo gets to the store he pulls out the list he made at home. He is cooking chili and wants to be sure he buys all of the ingredients he needs.

As Theo walks around the store and finds the items that are on his list, he checks off each one and puts it into his cart. He passes a bag of chips that looks super tasty. Theo picks them up and dreams of how crunchy and delicious they would taste, but he decides not to put the chips into his cart.

Today, Theo is only buying things that are on his list because he does not want to waste any money. When he has checked each item off of his list, Theo gets in line to check out.

Part A: Check Each Box as you Complete the Task

❑   **Read the Story**
❑   **Circle the word (list) in the story**
❑   **Trace & Write the word below:**

list   -----------------------   -----------------------

Part B: Fill in the Blank

1. **Who is the story about?**

_____

2. **Why does Theo use a list when he shops?**

_____

_____

Part C: Write the Main Idea of the Story

_____

_____

_____

_____

_____

Part D: Write One Supporting Detail from the Story

_____

_____

_____

_____

_____

Part E: Deepen your Understanding

Which item did Theo put back?	What is Theo making?
a. Cookies	a. Chips
b. Sourdough Bread	b. Chili
c. Chips	c. Pizza
d. Soda	d. Lasagna

List two ways making a list and using it while you shop can be helpful.

_____

_____

_____

_____

_____

_____

_____

_____

_____

_____

_____

_____

_____

My sketch of a grocery list:

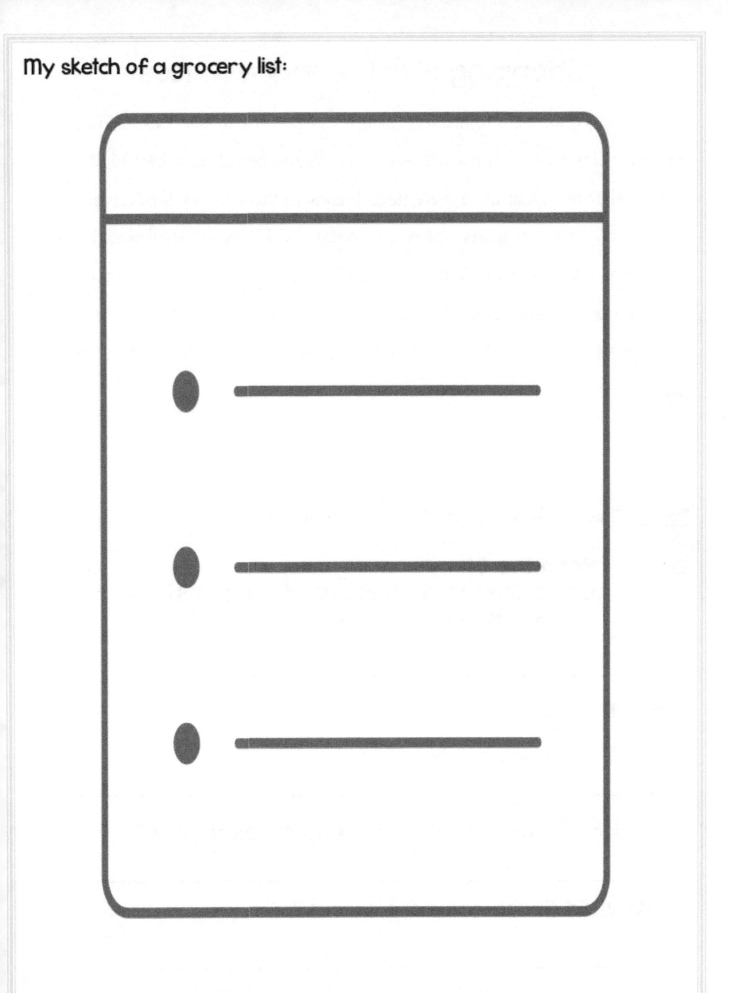

Shopping Skill: Compare Prices

Grace went to the store with a very short list. She was making marshmallow treats and needed three ingredients; cereal, marshmallows and butter. She found that there were three brands of the same kind of cereal.

Grace compared the prices to see which box of cereal was the least expensive. She wanted to save as much of her money as possible. Grace chose the plain brown box of cereal. She liked the look of the colorful box better, but she wanted to save as much money as possible. The plain box was the least expensive.

Part A: Check Each Box as you Complete the Task

❑   **Read the Story**
❑   **Circle the word** compared **in the story**
❑   **Trace & Write the word below:**

compared _____

Part B: Fill in the Blank

1. Who is the story about?

_____

2. Which box of cereal was the least expensive?

_____

3. Why did Grace compare prices?

_____

Part C: Write the Main Idea of the Story

_____

_____

_____

_____

Part D: Write One Supporting Detail from the Story

_____

_____

_____

_____

Part E: Deepen your Understanding

What is Grace making?

a. Cookies

b. Marshmallow Treats

c. Popsicles

d. Dinner

Which of these ingredients was not on Grace's list?

a. Sprinkles

b. Marshmallows

c. Cereal

d. Butter

Shopping Skill: Compare Prices

Ian was looking for a large bag of flour to bake cookies for his class bake sale. He wanted to buy as much flour as he could afford. Ian found one bag of flour for $3 and another for $2.

At first, Ian thought he would buy the $2 bag since it cost less money. Then he noticed that the bag only had 5 ounces of flour in it. The $3 bag cost more money but it had 10 ounces of flour in it!

Ian decided to spend a little more money to get twice the amount of flour. He knows that when you are comparing prices it is important to pay attention to how much is in each package as well as how much the item costs.

Part A: Check Each Box as you Complete the Task

❏ **Read the Story**
❏ **Circle the word** prices **in the story**
❏ **Trace & Write the word below:**

prices _____   _____

Part B: Fill in the Blank

1. **Who is the story about?**

_____

2. **Why is Ian buying flour?**

_____

3. **Which bag of flour did Ian buy?**

_____

Part C: Write the Main Idea of the Story

_____

_____

_____

_____

_____

Part D: Write One Supporting Detail from the Story

_____

_____

_____

_____

_____

Part E How did comparing prices save Ian money?

_____

_____

_____

_____

_____

_____

_____

_____

_____

What does it mean to compare prices? How might it help you save money when shopping for groceries?

_____

_____

_____

_____

_____

_____

_____

_____

_____

_____

_____

_____

My sketch of two similar items with different prices:

163

Shopping Skill: Stay within a Budget

Colton never goes to the store without a list and a budget. His list tells him what he needs to buy. Usually, he buys ingredients to make healthy dinners for the week. His budget tells him how much money he is able to spend on food.

Colton knows that staying within a budget is the most important way to save money at the grocery store. He wants to buy a bag of sour gummies while he is there. So, Colton makes sure he saves $1.75 in his budget to pay for the candy and adds the sour gummies to his shopping list. This way, Colton can buy treats for himself as well as the groceries that he needs for the week.

Part A: Check Each Box as you Complete the Task

❑ Read the Story
❑ Circle the word (budget) in the story
❑ Trace & Write the word below:

budget
_____   _____

Part B: Fill in the Blank

1. Who is the story about?

_____

2. What does Colton bring to the store?

_____

3. What is Colton buying at the store?

_____

Shopping Skill: Stay within a Budget

Part C: Write the Main Idea of the Story

_____

_____

_____

_____

_____

Part D: Write One Supporting Detail from the Story

_____

_____

_____

_____

_____

Part E: Deepen your Understanding

What does Colton's budget tell him?	What does Colton's list tell him?
_____	_____
_____	_____
_____	_____
_____	_____
_____	_____
_____	_____
_____	_____

Shopping Skill: Stay within a Budget

Natalie does not have very much money to spend on groceries. The small amount she does have needs to buy her enough food to eat breakfast for the entire week. So, when Natalie shops she sticks to a strict budget.

She uses the calculator on her phone to add up how much each item is as she puts it into her basket. This way, Natalie knows she will have enough money when she gets to the cash register. Natalie looks at the price tags, punches in the numbers, and adds a little extra to account for sales tax.

She is able to stay within her budget since she tallies the cost as she shops. Natalie always knows how much she has available to spend in her wallet and she makes sure that she can afford everything she puts into her cart.

Part A: Check Each Box as you Complete the Task

❑ **Read the Story**
❑ **Circle the word budget in the story**
❑ **Trace & Write the word below:**

budget
_____   _____

Part B: Fill in the Blank

1. **Who is the story about?**

   _____

2. **How does Natalie use the calculator on her phone?**

   _____

   _____

   _____

Shopping Skills: Stay within a Budget

Part C: Write the Main Idea of the Story

_____

_____

_____

_____

Part D: Write One Supporting Detail from the Story

_____

_____

_____

_____

Part E: Deepen your Understanding

What numbers does Natalie add on her calculator?

a. The price plus sales tax

b. Only the price

c. An estimate of the price

d. She does not add on her calculator

What does Natalie need to buy with her food budget?

a. Lunch for the week

b. Dinner for the week

c. Breakfast for the week

d. Snacks for the month

Why is it important to make a budget and stay within it when you shop?

_____

_____

_____

_____

_____

_____

_____

_____

_____

_____

_____

_____

My sketch of the ingredients I need to budget for in order to make a pizza:

Shopping Skill: Shop Politely

On the day before the big holiday, the store was crowded. Everyone was shopping and filling their carts with last minute gifts for friends and family. Lines were long and people were pushy.

Hunter wanted to buy his brother the Running Robot video game as a gift. By the time he made it to the aisle, the store was completely out! He could not believe it. Hunter got in line to ask the customer service representative when they would get more. He knew that he would have to make a big effort to be patient and understanding when talking to them.

Hunter took a deep breath and tried to enjoy the hustle and bustle of the store. Being polite helps everyone have a better experience. When it was finally his turn, Hunter smiled politely and asked his question.

Part A: Check Each Box as you Complete the Task

❑   **Read the Story**
❑   **Circle the word (politely) in the story**
❑   **Trace & Write the word below:**

politely
_____   _____

Part B: Fill in the Blank

1. **Who is the story about?**

_____

2. **Describe the atmosphere of the store.**

_____

3. **Who is Hunter shopping for?**

_____

Part C: Write the Main Idea of the Story

_____

_____

_____

_____

Part D: Write One Supporting Detail from the Story

_____

_____

_____

_____

Part E Why did Hunter need to be extra patient when talking to the customer service person?

_____

_____

_____

_____

_____

_____

_____

_____

171

Shopping Skill: Shop Politely

Amelia is going on a shopping outing to a clothing store with her class. Her goal is to shop politely while she searches for one pair of pants that fit her well.

Amelia will be polite by saying please and thank you. She will make eye contact with the people around her while she is in the store. Usually, Amelia likes to walk through stores with her head down checking her phone, and listening to music loudly but she knows that it is more polite to interact with the people around her. Amelia is making an effort to work towards her goal of shopping politely today.

Part A: Check Each Box as you Complete the Task

❑ Read the Story
❑ Circle the word (politely) in the story
❑ Trace & Write the word below:

___politely___ _____

Part B: Fill in the Blank

1. Who is the story about?

_____

2. Where is she going?

_____

3. What is hoping to buy?

_____

Part C: Write the Main Idea of the Story

_____

_____

_____

_____

_____

Part D: Write One Supporting Detail from the Story

_____

_____

_____

_____

_____

Part E Why is it polite to interact with the people around you at a store?

_____

_____

_____

_____

_____

_____

_____

_____

_____

_____

Why is it important to count your change?

_____

_____

_____

_____

_____

_____

_____

_____

_____

_____

_____

_____

My sketch of myself shopping politely:

Shopping Skill: Pay for Items

Adrian is working on his math skills and wants to learn how to pay for his own items at the grocery store. He uses a list and adds up items as he shops. Still, Adrian cannot help but to feel a little nervous every time he gets up to the cashier.

One thing that always helps Adrian feel more confident is counting his money before he leaves for the grocery store. This way his money is organized and he knows he has enough. When Adrian pays and gets change back, he is sure to put it straight into his wallet. This way he can find it the next time he goes grocery shopping.

Part A: Check Each Box as you Complete the Task

❑ **Read the Story**
❑ **Circle the word (pay) in the story**
❑ **Trace & Write the word below:**

pay _____   _____

Part B: Fill in the Blank

1. **Who is the story about?**

   _____

2. **What makes Adrian feel nervous?**

   _____

3. **Where does Adrian keep his change?**

   _____

Part C: Write the Main Idea of the Story

_____

_____

_____

_____

_____

Part D: Write One Supporting Detail from the Story

_____

_____

_____

_____

_____

Part E What does Adrian do before going to the store that helps him feel more confident when paying for his items?

_____

_____

_____

_____

_____

_____

_____

_____

Shopping Skill: Pay for Items

Layla thinks the absolute worst part of going shopping for clothing is making small talk with the cashier when you pay. Making small talk means chatting with the people you come in contact with without talking about anything important. Usually, people make small talk about things like the weather or a sports team.

Sometimes it can feel awkward, especially if you do not know what to say. Layla thinks of a few things she can say to make small talk with the cashier. When it is her turn to pay for her items, Layla asks the cashier whether or not she is enjoying the beautiful sunshine outside. The cashier smiles and answers Layla's question cheerfully. Layla is working on feeling more comfortable with small talk.

Part A: Check Each Box as you Complete the Task

❑   **Read the Story**
❑   **Circle the word (talk) in the story**
❑   **Trace & Write the word below:**

talk
-------------------------   -------------------------

Part B: Fill in the Blank

1. **Who is the story about?**

   _____

2. **What does Layla like the least about shopping?**

   _____

3. **What question does Layla ask the cashier?**

   _____

Part C: Write the Main Idea of the Story

_____

_____

_____

_____

_____

Part D: Write One Supporting Detail from the Story

_____

_____

_____

_____

Part E What is small talk?

_____

_____

_____

_____

_____

_____

_____

_____

_____

How can making small talk help you become a more polite shopper?

_____

_____

_____

_____

_____

_____

_____

_____

_____

_____

_____

_____

_____

_____

My sketch of a few topics that make good "small talk":

Shopping Skills

Check point! Review each skill.

- ☐ Use a List
- ☐ Compare Prices
- ☐ Stay within a Budget
- ☐ Shop Politely
- ☐ Pay for Items

Here is what I know about going shopping:

My favorite place to shop:

One shopping skill I am already good at is...

Shopping Skills I need to Practice are:

- ○
- ○
- ○
- ○
- ○
- ○
- ○

Next time I go shopping I will...

When I need groceries, I can shop at...

Think about your shopping outing. How did you do?

Rate yourself on each skill you practiced while you were there.

SKILL	5 Points	3 Points	1 Point
Used a List	○ Made a list before going ○ Brought list to the store ○ Checked off items ○ Only purchased items on the list	○ Made a list at the store ○ Bought some items from the list ○ Added many items that were not on the list	○ Did not make a list ○ Purchased random items
Compared Prices	○ Looked at different brands of each item to purchase at the best price ○ Considered the price per ounce of each product	○ Looked at different brands of each item ○ Purchased the lowest priced package regardless of ounces in the container	○ Purchased the item with the best package regardless of price
Stayed within my budget	○ Used my list ○ Added up prices as I shopped ○ Knew exactly how much money I had available to spend	○ Purchased some items from my list ○ Estimated how much each item was as I shopped ○ Knew "about" how much I could spend	○ Did not use my list ○ Did not check prices or add up the cost as I shopped ○ Guessed whether or not I would have enough money
Shopped Politely	○ Walked ○ Said excuse me, please and thanks ○ Smiled when I made eye contact ○ Waited patiently	○ Walked quickly ○ Reached in front of people ○ Some eye contact ○ Waited my turn	○ Ran or jumped ○ Impatient ○ No eye contact ○ Unpleasant
Paid for my Items	○ Money organized, out & ready ○ Made small talk with cashier ○ Counted my change ○ Polite	○ Brought enough money ○ Smiled at cashier ○ Took my change	○ Did not bring enough money ○ Silent while checking out ○ Did not take my change

Student Name:

Today, I feel I earned
Total Points: _____ /25

Looking at my rubric I see...

_____

_____

_____

_____

_____

_____

It is important to learn how to shop responsibly because...

I am proud of:

_____

_____

_____

_____

_____

_____

_____

_____

I need to keep working on:

_____

_____

_____

_____

_____

_____

Community Based Instruction

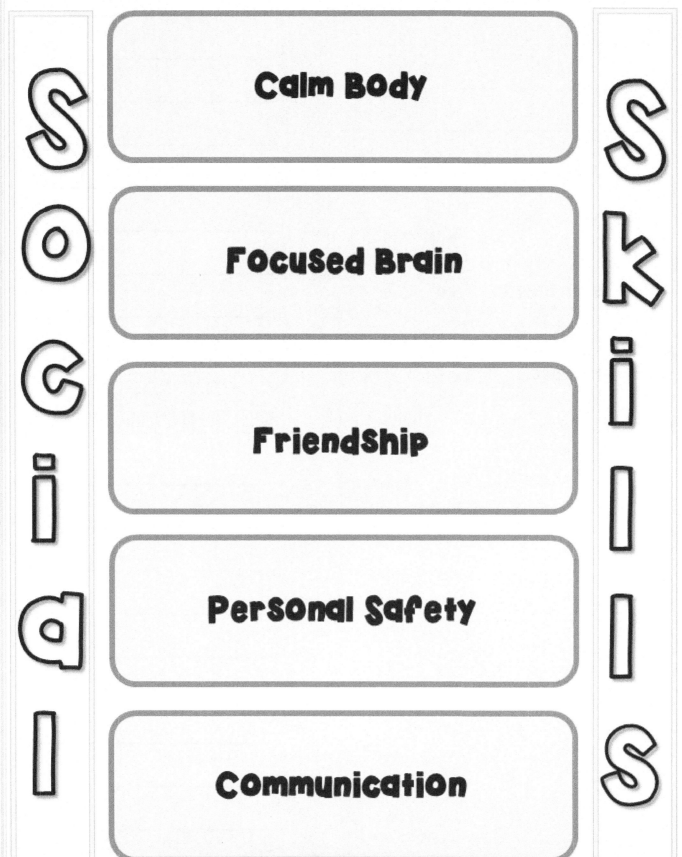

S O c i a l

Calm Body

Focused Brain

FriendShip

PerSonal Safety

Communication

S k i l l s

Community Based Instruction

Warm Up: Social Skills

What is a social skill?

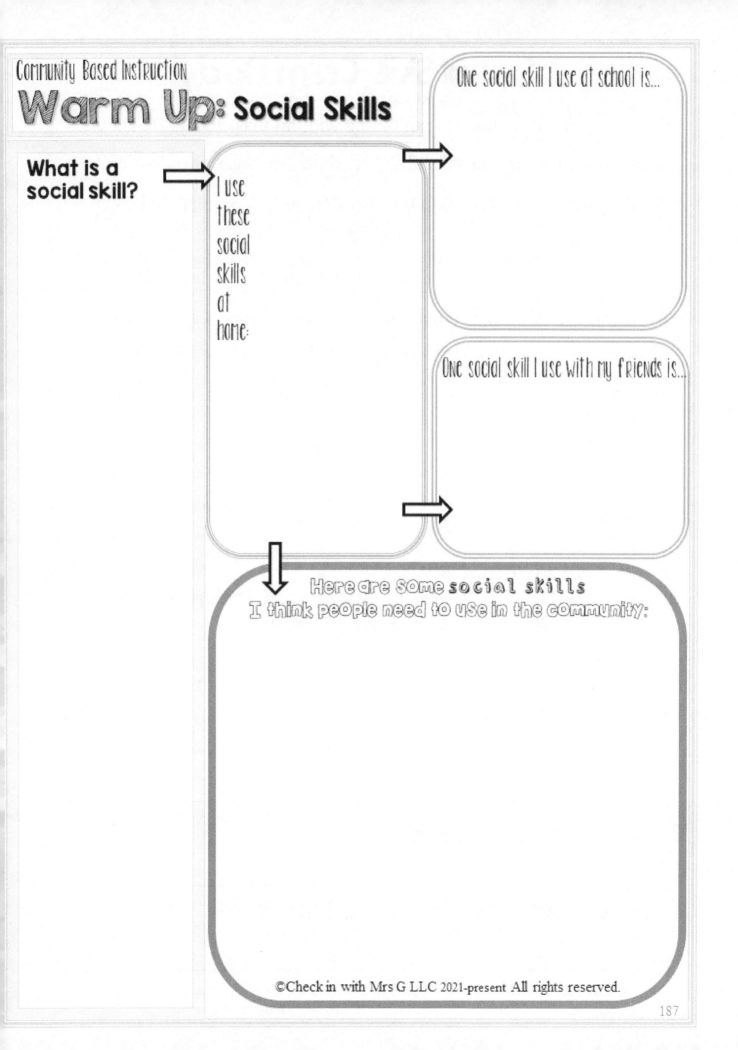

I use these social skills at home:

One social skill I use at school is...

One social skill I use with my friends is...

Here are some social skills
I think people need to use in the community:

187

Social Skill: Calm Body

Aaron is going on an outing with his class today. He knows wants to focus on his social skills. Last time they went on an outing, Aaron got in trouble because he ran into Duane when he was supposed to be walking calmly.

Aaron knows that it is important to keep his body calm and under control when he is out in the community. Aaron wants to be safe and he wants other people to feel safe around him. So, today Aaron is making it his goal to have a calm body and to keep his hands to himself while he is on his outing with his class.

Part A: Check Each Box as you Complete the Task

☐   **Read the Story**
☐   **Circle the word** (body) **in the story**
☐   **Trace & Write the word below:**

body

_____   _____

Part B: Fill in the Blank

1. **Who is this story about?**

   _____

2. **Where is Aaron going?**

   _____

3. **What is Aaron's goal during his outing?**

   _____

Part C: Write the Main Idea of the Story

_____

_____

_____

_____

_____

Part D: Write One Supporting Detail from the Story

_____

_____

_____

_____

_____

Part E: Deepen your Understanding

Who did Aaron run into during his last outing?	How does Aaron want other people to feel when they are around him?
a. His teacher	
b. Duane	
c. Emily	
d. A stranger	

Social Skill: Calm Body

Savannah is on an outing with her class. They are going to help at an elementary school in the kindergarten classroom. She is so excited!

Savannah knows that she needs to set a good example so she will be sure to keep her body under control. Savannah will make eye contact with people when they talk to her and she will take deep breaths if she gets too excited. Savannah wants to help out by reading to the kinder students. Having a calm body will show her teacher that she is responsible enough to work with young students.

Part A: Check Each Box as you Complete the Task

❑ **Read the Story**
❑ **Circle the word** (body) **in the story**
❑ **Trace & Write the word below:**

body
------------------------------   ------------------------------

Part B: Fill in the Blank

1. **Who is this story about?**

_____

2. **Where is Savannah's class going?**

_____

3. **What will Savannah do in the kindergarten classroom?**

_____

Part C: Write the Main Idea of the Story

_____

_____

_____

_____

_____

Part D: Write One Supporting Detail from the Story

_____

_____

_____

_____

_____

Part E: What does it look like to set a good example for a younger student?

_____

_____

_____

_____

_____

_____

_____

How can having a calm body during a community outing keep you and others safe?

_____

_____

_____

_____

_____

_____

_____

_____

_____

_____

_____

_____

My sketch of what a calm body looks like:

Social Skill: Focused Brain

Eleanor is working on focusing when she is out in the community. Her mom mentioned that Eleanor seems gets distracted every time they are shopping. Today, Eleanor and her mom are shopping at Terri's Shop looking for a winter coat.

Eleanor sees an amazing sequin purse runs towards it. She wanders away from her mom. Eleanor's mom is frustrated. She asks Eleanor to come back and focus on what they shopping for. Eleanor knows that she can do it! She will focus on finding a coat. If Eleanor sees something else that is interesting, she will ask her mom if it is ok to quickly go look at it.

Part A: Check Each Box as you Complete the Task

- ☐ **Read the Story**
- ☐ **Circle the word** (focus) **in the story**
- ☐ **Trace & Write the word below:**

focus
_____   _____

Part B: Fill in the Blank

1. **Who is this story about?**

   _____

2. **What skill is Eleanor working on?**

   _____

3. **Who is Eleanor shopping with?**

   _____

Part C: Write the Main Idea of the Story

_____

_____

_____

_____

_____

Part D: Write One Supporting Detail from the Story

_____

_____

_____

_____

_____

Part E: Deepen your Understanding

What was Eleanor shopping for?	Why do you think Eleanor's mom is feeling frustrated?
a. Winter hat	_____
b. Coat	_____
c. Gloves	_____
d. Rain boots	_____

Social Skill: Focused Brain

Today is an exciting day for William. He will be going to work for the first time. William is going with his class to work at a coffee shop. He will be trained on how to use some of the machines.

William wants to be a good employee so he knows it is important to understand exactly what he needs to do. He will focus on what his new boss is saying and he will ask questions about anything he does not understand. William knows that as long as his questions are on topic his boss will not mind explaining them.

Part A: Check Each Box as you Complete the Task

☐ Read the Story
☐ Circle the word ⟨understand⟩ in the story
☐ Trace & Write the word below:

understand _____

Part B: Fill in the Blank

1. Who is this story about?

_____

2. Why is William excited?

_____

3. Where will William work?

_____

Part C: Write the Main Idea of the Story

_____

_____

_____

_____

_____

Part D: Write One Supporting Detail from the Story

_____

_____

_____

_____

_____

Part E: Deepen your Understanding

What is William being trained on?	Why is it important for William to ask questions?
a. Taking out the trash	_____
	_____
b. Using the coffee machines	_____
	_____
c. Cleaning the counters	_____
	_____
d. Refilling the containers	_____
	_____

Why is it a good idea to focus on a social skills goal during a community outing?

_____

_____

_____

_____

_____

_____

_____

_____

_____

_____

_____

_____

My sketch of an outing in the community:

Social Skill: Friendship

Noah is working with his classmates on a project to help clean up the park close to their school. Before they left, their teacher asked him to focus on his friendship skills while they are working.

Noah likes to work fast. He is a hard worker and he gets things done. But sometimes, people do not like to work with him. Noah is not good at listening to other people's opinions or including them in making decisions. While they are on their outing, Noah will try to focus on being a good friend and working as a part of the team instead of doing everything by himself.

If he can manage to work with others, he will get more accomplished and people will want to work with him. Noah is learning more about friendship and working as a part of a team.

Part A: Check Each Box as you Complete the Task

❑ Read the Story
❑ Circle the word ⟨friendship⟩ in the story
❑ Trace & Write the word below:

friendship _____ _____

Part B: Fill in the Blank

I. Who is this story about?

_____

2. What project is Noah's class working on?

_____

3. What social skill is Noah focusing on?

_____

Part C: Write the Main Idea of the Story

_____

_____

_____

_____

_____

Part D: Write One Supporting Detail from the Story

_____

_____

_____

_____

_____

Part E: Deepen your Understanding

Who asked Noah to focus on friendship skills during the outing?	What is one friendship skill that Noah is practicing?
a. His mom b. Himself c. His teacher d. His classmates	_____ _____ _____ _____ _____ _____ _____ _____

Social Skill: Friendship

During her outing to the library, Addison and her friends focused on being kind and respectful to everyone. They smiled, made eye contact, and responded when people made small talk with them.

Addison and her friends wanted to make other people feel comfortable. Having a close friendship was wonderful but it didn't mean that they could ignore everyone else.

Addison asked the librarian for help with finding a good book about mermaids. Then, she asked the barista at the coffee stand how his day was going. Addison and her friends are working on social skills. They are learning to include everyone.

Part A: Check Each Box as you Complete the Task

❑ **Read the Story**
❑ **Circle the word** ⟨ friends ⟩ **in the story**
❑ **Trace & Write the word below:**

friends
-------------------------   -------------------------

Part B: Fill in the Blank

1. **Who is this story about?**

_____

2. **What social skill is Addison working on?**

_____

3. **How does Addison try to include others?**

_____

Part C: Write the Main Idea of the Story

_____

_____

_____

_____

_____

Part D: Write One Supporting Detail from the Story

_____

_____

_____

_____

_____

Part E: Deepen your Understanding

What kind of book was Addison looking for?

a. Werewolf

b. Vampire

c. Dragon

d. Mermaid

Who did Addison not chat with during her outing to the library?

a. The librarian

b. The barista

c. The bus driver

d. Her friends

List three ways you can be a good friend to a classmate during a community outing.

_____

_____

_____

_____

_____

_____

_____

_____

_____

_____

_____

_____

_____

_____

My sketch of me with my friends on an outing in our community:

Social Skill: Personal Safety

Naia is getting ready for her class outing to the zoo. She wants to make sure she is safe and prepared for the trip. Naia makes sure to wear a jacket since the weather forecast mentioned that it might rain. She considers wearing her new shoes with straps but decides to wear her running shoes since there are a lot of hills at the zoo.

Naia brings her cell phone completely charged and is sure to stay with the group. This way she can focus on having fun and enjoying the animals, especially the monkeys. Planning ahead is a great way for Naia to keep herself safe and prepared!

Part A: Check Each Box as you Complete the Task

- ☐ Read the Story
- ☐ Circle the word ⟨prepared⟩ in the story
- ☐ Trace & Write the word below:

prepared _____   _____

Part B: Fill in the Blank

1. Who is this story about?

_____

2. What outing is Naia preparing for?

_____

3. What will Naia focus on while she is at the zoo?

_____

Part C: Write the Main Idea of the Story

_____

_____

_____

_____

_____

Part D: Write One Supporting Detail from the Story

_____

_____

_____

_____

_____

Part E: Make a list of the things Naia did to prepare for her class outing to the zoo.

_____

_____

_____

_____

_____

_____

_____

_____

_____

Social Skill: Personal Safety

Elias is learning how much information to share with strangers when he is in the community. Elias knows that making small talk about things like the weather is totally appropriate. He would never share personal details like where he lives or where he goes to school.

Elias sticks to safe topics like the weather or the latest TV shows. If anyone presses him to share more information than he feels comfortable with he walks away from the conversation. Elias is learning to be friendly while keeping himself safe.

Part A: Check Each Box as you Complete the Task

❑   **Read the Story**
❑   **Circle the word** (safe) **in the story**
❑   **Trace & Write the word below:**

safe

-------------------------   -------------------------

Part B: Fill in the Blank

1. **Who is this story about?**

    _____

2. **What is a good topic to use when making small talk?**

    _____

3. **Write one thing Elias would not share with a stranger.**

    _____

Part C: Write the Main Idea of the Story

_____

_____

_____

_____

_____

Part D: Write One Supporting Detail from the Story

_____

_____

_____

_____

_____

Part E: Why does Elias think it's unsafe to share where he lives with a stranger?

_____

_____

_____

_____

_____

_____

_____

_____

_____

What is one way you can use technology to keep yourself safe during a community outing?

_____

_____

_____

_____

_____

_____

_____

_____

_____

_____

_____

My sketch of myself being safe in the community:

Social Skill: Communication

One of the best ways to make people feel comfortable is to ask questions about something they are interested in. Ariana is trying to welcome a new student, Desiree to her class. She notices that Desiree has a backpack with a unicorn on it.

Even though Arianna is not interested in unicorns she decides to start a conversation with Desiree by asking, "What do you like about unicorns?" Desiree smiles brightly and looks up for the first time since sitting down at the table. Arianna is happy that she is able to get Desiree to open up and feel comfortable at her new school.

Part A: Check Each Box as you Complete the Task

❑   Read the Story
❑   Circle the word comfortable in the story
❑   Trace & Write the word below:

comfortable   --------------------------   --------------------------

Part B: Fill in the Blank

1. Who is this story about?

_____

2. What clue made Arianna think Desiree might be interested in unicorns?

_____

_____

_____

_____

Part C: Write the Main Idea of the Story

_____

_____

_____

_____

_____

Part D: Write One Supporting Detail from the Story

_____

_____

_____

_____

_____

Part E: Why did Arianna ask Desiree a question about unicorns even though Arianna is not interested unicorns?

_____

_____

_____

_____

_____

_____

_____

_____

_____

Social Skill: Communication

When Liam is out in the community, his goal is to focus on his communication skills. He is heading to a convention where he will meet some of his favorite online content creators. Liam can hardly wait!

He loves watching videos online and would someday like to start his own channel. Liam wants to make a good impression on everyone he meets at the convention.

He will have open body language for example, not crossing his arms and making eye contact. He will ask questions and smile in a friendly way. Liam hopes to grab a selfie with a few people while he is there and share the pictures on his own social media pages.

Part A: Check Each Box as you Complete the Task

❑   Read the Story
❑   Circle the word (communication) in the story
❑   Trace & Write the word below:

communication   ------------------------------

Part B: Fill in the Blank

I. Who is this story about?

_____

2. What kind of convention is Liam going to?

_____

3. What goal is Liam focusing on while he is there?

_____

Part C: Write the Main Idea of the Story

_____

_____

_____

_____

Part D: Write One Supporting Detail from the Story

_____

_____

_____

_____

Part E: Deepen your Understanding

Why is Liam excited about the convention?	What will Liam do to make a good impression on the people he meets?
a. He loves online videos and hopes to have his own channel	
b. He loves to be around new people	
c. He wants to take a day off of school	

How can you use body language to communicate
with strangers while you are in the community?

_____

_____

_____

_____

_____

_____

_____

_____

_____

_____

_____

_____

_____

My sketch of a convention I would like to attend:

Social Skills

Check point! Review each skill.

- ☐ Calm Body
- ☐ Focused Brain
- ☐ Friendship
- ☐ Personal Safety
- ☐ Communication

Here is what I know about using social skills on community outings:

A Social Skill I am an expert at is:

One social skill I am already good at is...

Make a Connection

Social Skills I need to Practice:

○

○

○

○

○

○

○

Positive social skills sound like...

Social skills are important because...

Think about your social skills during the last outing. How did you do?

Rate yourself on each skill you practiced while you were there.

Date:

Outing:

SKILL	5 Points	3 Points	1 Point
Body	○ Calm ○ Focused ○ Listened ○ Hands to self ○ Eye contact	○ A little excited ○ Mostly focused ○ Listened with reminders ○ Hands to self with reminders ○ Some eye contact	○ Wild ○ Unfocused ○ Not listening ○ Touching others ○ No eye contact
Brain	○ Paid attention ○ Gave my best effort ○ Asked for help when I needed it ○ Asked on topic questions	○ Paid attention with some reminders ○ Gave some effort ○ Accepted help when it was offered ○ Asked questions that were off topic	○ Did not pay attention ○ No effort shown ○ Did not ask for help ○ Did not accept help ○ Did not ask questions
Friendship	○ Made others feel comfortable ○ Worked as a part of a team ○ Kind ○ Respectful to everyone	○ Made others feel somewhat comfortable ○ Did some work as a part of a team ○ Mostly kind ○ Respectful to some	○ Made others uncomfortable ○ Did not work with a team ○ Unkind ○ Disrespectful
Personal Safety	○ Wore appropriate clothes for the weather ○ Aware of surroundings ○ Stayed with the group ○ Friendly without sharing too much personal information	○ Wore mostly appropriate clothes for the weather ○ Somewhat aware of surroundings ○ Usually stayed with group ○ Shared some personal information	○ Wore inappropriate clothes for the weather ○ Not aware of surroundings ○ Left the group ○ Overshared personal information
Communication	○ Respectful words ○ Open body language ○ Asked questions about other people	○ Mostly respectful words ○ Some open body language ○ Responded to questions	○ Disrespectful words ○ Closed body language ○ Did not ask or respond to questions

Student Name:

Today, I feel I earned

Total Points: ___/25

Looking at my rubric I see...

It is
important
to practice
social skills
in the community
because...

I am proud of:

_____

_____

_____

_____

_____

_____

_____

_____

I need to keep working on:

_____

_____

_____

_____

_____

_____

_____

_____

Community Based Instruction
Self Assessment Rubrics Blackline Masters

Think about your outing to the restaurant. How did you do?

Rate yourself on each skill you practiced while you were there.

Date:

Restaurant Name:

SKILL	5 Points	3 Points	1 Point
Entered the Restaurant Respectfully	○ Walked calmly ○ Used eye contact ○ Inside voice volume ○ Waited patiently ○ Friendly	○ Walked quickly ○ Some eye contact ○ Talked loudly ○ Waited ○ Somewhat friendly	○ Ran ○ No eye contact ○ Yelled or was disruptive ○ Impatient ○ Unfriendly
Read the Menu	○ Opened the menu ○ Read the list of items ○ Chose an item independently ○ Evaluated cost & stayed within budget	○ Opened the menu with reminders ○ Asked for an item without checking the menu ○ Chose an item with support ○ Chose something I could not afford	○ Did not look at the menu ○ Asked an adult to choose food ○ Did not consider the cost
Ordered my Food	○ Made eye contact ○ Spoke clearly ○ Appropriate volume ○ Extremely polite (said Please/ Thank You)	○ Some eye contact ○ Order was unclear ○ Spoke too quietly or too loudly ○ Somewhat polite	○ No eye contact ○ Did not order on my own ○ Impolite or demanding
Paid for my Food	○ Had my money organized & ready ○ Gave an appropriate amount ○ Counted my change ○ Kept my receipt in a safe place	○ Had my money ○ Gave an amount larger than what was owed ○ Took my change ○ Took my receipt	○ Forgot my money ○ Gave less than what was owed ○ Did not take my change ○ Did not take my receipt
Left Politely	○ Walked calmly ○ Used eye contact ○ Inside voice volume ○ Said thank you ○ Friendly ○ Held the door open for someone	○ Walked quickly ○ Some eye contact ○ Talked loudly ○ Said thank you ○ Somewhat friendly	○ Ran ○ No eye contact ○ Yelled or was disruptive ○ Unfriendly

Student Name:

Today, I feel I earned

Total Points: ____ /25

Student Rubric Reflection: Restaurant

Looking at my rubric I see...

It is **important** to learn what to do at a **restaurant** because...

I am proud of:

_____

_____

_____

_____

_____

_____

_____

I need to keep working on:

_____

_____

_____

_____

_____

_____

Think about your community center outing. How did you do?

Rate yourself on each skill you practiced while you were there.

SKILL	5 Points	3 Points	1 Point
Exercise	o Participated willingly in individual or group exercise o Stretched out before & after o Drank water	o Unwillingly participated in individual or group exercise o Stretched out before or after o Drank water with prompts from an adult	o Did not participate in exercise o Did not drink water
Participation	o Made an effort to get involved o Played a game, sport or took a class o Positive attitude o Open body language	o Made an effort to get involved with adult prompts o Played a game, sport or took a class when invited o Mostly positive attitude o Mostly open body language	o Made no effort to get involved o Did not play a game, sport or take a class o Negative attitude o Closed body language
Connection	o Reviewed list of activities to find a group or class of interest o Sought out peers to collaborate on activities o Engaged with new peers	o Reviewed list of activities with help from an adult o Collaborated on activities o Responded to new peers	o Did not investigate new activities o Played/worked alone o Did not respond to new peers
Interests	o Started conversations about things I find interesting o Started conversations about things others find interesting o Asked questions about other's interests	o Participated in conversations about things I find interesting o Responded to questions about my interests	o Did not participate in conversations about interests o Did not ask questions or respond to other's questions
Events	o Asked questions about upcoming events o Made a plan to attend an upcoming event o Willing to try new activity	o Read about upcoming events o Showed an interest in attending events o Willing to try new activity with adult support	o Did not show an interest in attending events o Unwilling to try new activity

Student Name:

Today, I feel I earned

Total Points: _____ /25

Looking at my rubric I see...

It is
important
to get involved
in my
community
center
because...

I am proud of:

_____

_____

_____

_____

_____

_____

_____

I need to keep working on:

_____

_____

_____

_____

_____

_____

_____

Think about your outing on public transportation. How did you do?

Rate yourself on each skill you practiced while you were there.

SKILL	5 Points	3 Points	1 Point
Found the Bus Stop	○ Researched where the bus stops prior to leaving ○ Walked on sidewalks ○ Crossed the street using crosswalks	○ Worked with an adult or map to find the bus stop ○ Walked on sidewalks with reminders ○ Crossed the street safely	○ Followed an adult to the bus stop ○ Walked in the street ○ Crossed streets unsafely
Got on the Correct Bus	○ Arrived a few minutes early ○ Read the routes map to find which bus to get on ○ Waited patiently ○ Waited safely out of the street	○ Arrived on time ○ Asked an adult which bus to get on ○ Waited ○ Stayed out of the street with adult support	○ Missed the bus ○ Was unsure of which bus to get on ○ Impatient ○ Stood/walked into the street
Paid or Used my Bus Pass	○ Had money or pass organized, out & ready ○ Put pass or change safely back into wallet ○ Friendly to the driver	○ Had money or pass ○ Took pass or change ○ Made eye contact with the driver	○ Forgot money or pass ○ Did not take change or pass after boarding ○ Unfriendly to the driver
Rode the Bus Safely	○ Walked onto the bus ○ Found a seat quickly or stood holding on ○ Kept my belongings safely with me ○ Stayed aware of my surroundings	○ Walked quickly onto the bus ○ Searched for the perfect seat or stood leaning against pole ○ Put my belongings on a seat near me ○ Looked around every ○ once in awhile	○ Ran, hopped or leapt onto the bus ○ Passed many open seats or stood without holding on ○ Put my belongings on the floor
Got Off of the Bus Appropriately	○ Pulled the stop request cord right before my stop ○ Gathered my belongings ahead of time ○ Walked to the door	○ Pulled the stop request cord when we passed my stop ○ Gathered my belongings after we stopped ○ Walked fast to the door	○ Did not pull the stop request cord ○ Left my belongings ○ Ran, hopped, or jumped to the door

Student Name:

Today, I feel I earned

Total Points: ___ /25

Looking at my rubric I see...

I am proud of:

_____

_____

_____

_____

_____

_____

_____

_____

It is important to learn how to use public transportation because...

I need to keep working on:

_____

_____

_____

_____

_____

_____

_____

_____

Think about your library outing. How did you do?

Rate yourself on each skill you practiced while you were there.

SKILL	5 Points	3 Points	1 Point
Found Books of Interest	o Used computer system to locate a specific genre o Had 2 or more books or topics of interest in mind o Searched by author or title for specific books	o Asked librarian to locate a genre o Had a book or topic of interest in mind o Searched for a specific type book	o Looked randomly for books o Had no books or topics of interest in mind o Did not find an interesting book
Used the Computers	o Used library card to login independently o Accessed a specified website independently o Printed documents independently o Logged off independently	o Used library card to login with support o Accessed a specified website with support o Printed documents with support o Logged off with a prompt from an adult	o Unable to login o Attempted to access inappropriate content o Unable to print documents o Logged off with resistance or multiple prompts
Followed the Library Rules	o Quiet voice o Reshelf books in the correct locations o Walked o Respected others personal space	o Mostly quiet voice o Put books back on shelves in random locations o Walked quickly o Mostly respected others personal space	o Loud voice o Did not put books back on shelves o Ran, hopped or jumped o Invaded others personal space
Checked Out a Book	o Selected a high interested book o Selected a book with a reading level that was a good fit for me o Used my library card independently	o Selected a high interest book with support o Selected a book with a reading level that was almost a good fit for me o Used my library card with support	o Did not choose a book I am interested in o Selected a book with a too difficult or too simple reading level for me o Forgot or did not use my library card
Learned about Community Events	o Read about upcoming community events o Selected one that I would like to attend o Asked questions to the library staff about events	o Found upcoming community events listings o Considered whether or not I would like to attend any of them with prompts from an adult	o Did not locate the events listings o Uninterested in community events

Student Name:

Today, I feel I earned

Total Points: ___/25

Student Rubric Reflection: Library Skills

Looking at my rubric I see...

_____

_____

_____

_____

_____

_____

It is important to know how to use the library because...

I am proud of:

_____

_____

_____

_____

_____

_____

_____

I need to keep working on:

_____

_____

_____

_____

_____

_____

_____

Think about your shopping outing. How did you do?

Rate yourself on each skill you practiced while you were there.

Date:

Store Name:

SKILL	5 Points	3 Points	1 Point
Used a List	○ Made a list before going ○ Brought list to the store ○ Checked off items ○ Only purchased items on the list	○ Made a list at the store ○ Bought some items from the list ○ Added many items that were not on the list	○ Did not make a list ○ Purchased random items
Compared Prices	○ Looked at different brands of each item to purchase at the best price ○ Considered the price per ounce of each product	○ Looked at different brands of each item ○ Purchased the lowest priced package regardless of ounces in the container	○ Purchased the item with the best package regardless of price
Stayed within my budget	○ Used my list ○ Added up prices as I shopped ○ Knew exactly how much money I had available to spend	○ Purchased some items from my list ○ Estimated how much each item was as I shopped ○ Knew "about" how much I could spend	○ Did not use my list ○ Did not check prices or add up the cost as I shopped ○ Guessed whether or not I would have enough money
Shopped Politely	○ Walked ○ Said excuse me, please and thanks ○ Smiled when I made eye contact ○ Waited patiently	○ Walked quickly ○ Reached in front of people ○ Some eye contact ○ Waited my turn	○ Ran or jumped ○ Impatient ○ No eye contact ○ Unpleasant
Paid for my Items	○ Money organized, out & ready ○ Made small talk with cashier ○ Counted my change ○ Polite	○ Brought enough money ○ Smiled at cashier ○ Took my change	○ Did not bring enough money ○ Silent while checking out ○ Did not take my change

Student Name:

Today, I feel I earned
Total Points: _____ /25

Looking at my rubric I see...

It is **important** to learn how to **shop responsibly** because...

I am proud of:

_____

_____

_____

_____

_____

_____

_____

I need to keep working on:

_____

_____

_____

_____

_____

_____

_____

Think about your social skills during the last outing. How did you do?

Rate yourself on each skill you practiced while you were there.

Date:

Outing:

SKILL	5 Points	3 Points	1 Point
Body	○ Calm ○ Focused ○ Listened ○ Hands to self ○ Eye contact	○ A little excited ○ Mostly focused ○ Listened with reminders ○ Hands to self with reminders ○ Some eye contact	○ Wild ○ Unfocused ○ Not listening ○ Touching others ○ No eye contact
Brain	○ Paid attention ○ Gave my best effort ○ Asked for help when I needed it ○ Asked on topic questions	○ Paid attention with some reminders ○ Gave some effort ○ Accepted help when it was offered ○ Asked questions that were off topic	○ Did not pay attention ○ No effort shown ○ Did not ask for help ○ Did not accept help ○ Did not ask questions
Friendship	○ Made others feel comfortable ○ Worked as a part of a team ○ Kind ○ Respectful to everyone	○ Made others feel somewhat comfortable ○ Did some work as a part of a team ○ Mostly kind ○ Respectful to some	○ Made others uncomfortable ○ Did not work with a team ○ Unkind ○ Disrespectful
Personal Safety	○ Wore appropriate clothes for the weather ○ Aware of surroundings ○ Stayed with the group ○ Friendly without sharing too much personal information	○ Wore mostly appropriate clothes for the weather ○ Somewhat aware of surroundings ○ Usually stayed with group ○ Shared some personal information	○ Wore inappropriate clothes for the weather ○ Not aware of surroundings ○ Left the group ○ Overshared personal information
Communication	○ Respectful words ○ Open body language ○ Asked questions about other people	○ Mostly respectful words ○ Some open body language ○ Responded to questions	○ Disrespectful words ○ Closed body language ○ Did not ask or respond to questions

Student Name:

Today, I feel I earned

Total Points: ____ /25

Looking at my rubric I see...

It is **important** to practice **social skills** in the community because...

I am proud of:

_____

_____

_____

_____

_____

_____

_____

_____

I need to keep working on:

_____

_____

_____

_____

_____

_____

_____

Rating during CBI outings! **Month:** _____

Student Name: **Month Total:**

Rating	M	T	W	Th	F	M	T	W	Th	F	M	T	W	Th	F	M	T	W	Th	F	M	T	W	Th	F
25																									
20																									
15																									
10																									
5																									

CBI Monthly Progress Graph

Visit my Blog:

- checkinwithmrsg.org

Connect with Me:

- Email: checkinwithmrsgontpt@gmail.com
- Instagram: @checkinwithmrs_g
- Facebook: @checkinwithmrsgontpt

Made in the USA
Las Vegas, NV
26 February 2023